AS MUCH AS

한국 비속어

KOREAN SLANG

INVECTIVE AND EUPHEMISM
THE "INSIDERS GUIDE"

exile press

Table of Contents

Intro

ㄱ The Mutable Transgender Giuk

간지난다; 갈구다; 갑이다; 강추; 강남스타일; 개기다; 개드립; 겁나게; 고고씽; 고딩(초딩, 중딩, 대딩, 직딩); 고춧가루 뿌리다; 골때린다; 골초 or 끌초; 공주병; 구라까다; 구리다; 귀차니즘; 까리하다; 까다; 깔(따구); 꺄 or 꺅; 깝치다; 깡(다구); (확)깬다; 꺼져; 꽝이다; 꼬라지; 꼬라지나다; 꼬붕; 꼬지다; 꼴았다; 꼴통; 꼽사리 끼다; 꿀벅지; 꼽살리다

ㄴ The Annoyingly Nasal Niun

나발불다; 나비; 나이롱 환자; 나와바리; 낙동강 오리알; 낙하산; 낚다; 네똥 굵다; 날라리; 넨장맞을; 노가다; 노가리 까다; 눈깔이 삐었다; 눈탱이가 밤탱이 되다; 농땡이

ㄷ Digut's Depth Revealed

대가리; 대략난감; 대박이다; 돌아가시겠다; 돌싱; 돌직구; 돗대; 됐거든(요); 된장녀; 뒤땅까다; 뒷북치다; 따 (왕따, 은따, 전따); 따가리; 따먹다; 딱지 떼다; 땡땡이 치다; 땡잡다; 띠껍다

ㄹ Riul's Absence is a Mystery
ㅁ Two Lips Meet to Merge Complete

만먹다; 말리다; 말 까다; 맛이 갔다; 맞장뜨다; 몰카(지); 물이 좋다; 몽땅

ㅂ Babbling Biup, Buzzing Free

바가지 긁다; 밤새 달려; 바가지 쓰다; 반사; 방콕; 배째라; 100m 미인; 불매; 불금; 벼락치기; 불알친구; 불타는 고구마; 불어; 빈대붙다; ~빠; 빡세다; 빡돌다; 뽀대난다; 뽀록; 뽀리다; 뽕브라; 뽕빼다; 삐끼; 삥뜯다

ㅅ Slick, Scaly and Separate of Lip

사오정; 삽질하다; 새대가리; 시원하다; 새되다; 섹끈하다; 식후땡; 싸가지없다; 쌍수; 싸이숨 (P'sigh); 쌩까다; 쌩얼; 썰렁하다; 썸(타다)

ㅇ The Yin and Yang of Iung's Lyric

아다; 안물; 왜 씹어?; 안습; 야리다; 양다리; 양아치; 엄창 (엠창); 일짱; 여병추; 영계; 이빠이; 입이 싸다; 잉여; 임마

ㅈ Jammin' to a Jiut Jingle

작업; 잘 나가; 쥐뿔; 쥐꼬리만큼; 지못미; 진도 어디까지나갔어?; 짝퉁; 짱이다; 짬뽕; 짭새; 쩐다; 쪽팔리다; 쭉쭉빵빵

ㅊ Get Your Chi Charged

착하다; 철판깔다; 찬밥; 출튀

ㅋ Mockingly Clear and Cold

컨닝하다

ㅌ Tried and True, Tiut Withdrew

태클걸다; 토끼다; 토나오다; 팅기다

ㅍ The Power of Piup

88만원 세대; 퍼뜩; 폭탄이다; 품절(남/녀); 피봤어

ㅎ An End of Alphabet Comes

허접; 하의실종; 헐; 환장하다; 후까시 잡다; 흑역사

Dedication & Copyright

This manuscript is dedicated to ChangHyun, the *Mandeugi* of our book and inspiration for much of its mischievous nature...

이 책을 우리의 좋은 친구인 창현에게 바칩니다.
짓궂은 성격의 내용에 영감을 준 우리 책의 만득이...

* * *

ChangHyun-ah, ChangHyun-ah museo-un ChangHyun-ah
You rascal, you rogue, you naughty naysayer...
What wicked words are you using now?
ChangHyun-ah, ChangHyun-ah ggeun-jeok-han ChangHyun-ah

창현아, 창현아 무서운 창현아
장난꾸러기, 악당, 개구쟁이 반대론자...
지금은 또 어떤 고약한 말을 쓰고 있니?
창현아, 창현아 끈적한 창현아

Special thanks goes out to the many people who helped create, edit and design this new edition, as well as those kind backers from Indiegogo who helped me get it started! In particular, I would like to mention the generosity of our Associate Producer James Geraci, a true supporter of independent writing.

ISBN 978-89-962405-5-6 03700   (Formerly 978 89 962405 0 1 13700) [Korea]
ISBN 978-1-936342-50-1   (1st ed. 978-0-9801974-2-6) [USA]
eISBN 9781936342518
Korean Slang: As much as A Rat's Tail / 쥐꼬리만큼
Library of Congress Cataloging-in-Publication Data Liptak, Peter N.
As Much as a Rat's Tail / by Peter N. Liptak & Siwoo Lee. 2nd ed.
p.252 cm. 21.5
Includes index
LCCN 2009902042
ISBN 978-1-936342-50-1 (alk. paper)
1. Korean language – Slang. 2. Korean language – Education. 3. Language and culture. 4. Korean wit and humor
I. Title
LC Classification: PL913 .L57 2015
467/.09 21 KO 495.7834
Language Code: engkor

Exile Press

Exile Press LLC 2355 Fairview Avenue North, #191 Roseville, MN 55113
www.ExilePress.com

The Menu of Korean Slang

A classification system you can really sink your teeth into... Use these icons as a guide to understand where each expression comes from and when it should be used.

Rice
Use it everyday, for every meal, all the time – really!
밥 먹듯 쓰는 말

Panchan
A simple side dish for something to snack on (not for everyday use).
때때로 쓰는 말

Soju
Expressions used while drinking! Shoot the shit shooting shots!
술 마실 때 쓰는 말

The Kimchi Pot
Watch out! Spicy language and swearing!
매운(상스러운) 말 그리고 욕, 조심하세요!

Ddokboki
Something sexual to snack on... Salacious and sweet!
성적인 표현

Coffee
Konglish(ee) – imported into Korea from the West.
서양에서 유래된 외래 비속어, 콩글리쉬.

Sushi
Imported into Korea from Japan.
일본에서 유래된 비속어

Hakgyo
Stuff students say – from school daze to hakgyo haze.
학교에서 쓰는 말

Cast of Characters

Main Characters

The Guys			
ChangHyun	창현	the troublemaker, or "the Rat" (AKA Bong)
SiWoo	시우	a stone-cold, slang philosopher
Peter	피터	a slang-slinging voyageur (AKA JungSuk)
TaeYong	태용	a bold, brash, and popular, yet laid back 'dude'
WonDong	원동	loves girls, but he's all talk and no action
DongWon	동원	loves drinking and partying (AKA Migu)
Victor	빅터	the newbie, the Russian riddler, Gollum's cousin

The Girls			
SoYoon	소윤	she's sooooo smart, sooooo annoyingly smart
JiYoon	지윤	everyone's little sister, this chic loves fashion
Minji	민지	a rich girl who always shows up without her wallet
Arum	아름	open-minded, free-spirited and beautiful
MinHee	민희	a plain girl with a Cinderella complex
HeeYeon	희연	a traditional Korean girl, so proud & stubborn

The Mob of Supporting Characters

The 3 Stooges			
ByungShik	병식	weak and a little slow, but somehow lucky
KwangSung	광성	rushes in to danger and loses
HwaSeok	화석	a rock-headed & duplicitous army private

The Four Sea-sons			
Bom	봄	the salary man, father & husband (Spring)
YeoReum	여름	the cute daughter (Summer)
Kaeul	가을	the MILF, a career woman and supermom (Fall)
KyoWul	겨울	the good son of Spring (Winter)

Korean moms			
Ajumma1	아줌마1	an older married woman
Ajumma2	아줌마2	a second such married woman

Distinguished Guests			
SeungMan	승만	1st President of Korea (the Freedom fighter)
ChungHee	정희	3rd President of Korea (the Adamant Industrialist)
DooHwan	두환	5th President of Korea (the Mass Murderer)
DaeJung	대중	8th President of Korea (Sunshine Policy Apologist)
MyungBak	명박	10th President of Korea (Where's the Beef?)
GeunHye	근혜	11th President of Korea (The Dictator's Daughter)
Psy	싸이	the surprising poster boy of Korean culture
MinShik	민식	the star of the original 'Old Boy'
JiTae	지태	the other main actor in 'Old Boy'
Bill	빌	"Party on!"
Ted	테드	"Excellent!"
Robin	로빈	the put-upon side kick
Batman	배트맨	the main man (or so he says)
PC	PC	the clunky computer you should never buy
Mac	맥	the apple of my eye

Not Really Names			
HaPum	하품	a yawn (high school girl)
HanSum	한숨	a sigh (high school girl)
MyongTae	명태	Alaskan Pollack (the high school guy)
SaengTae	생태	Alaskan Pollack (his twin brother)
PaJeon	파전	a Korean pancake (YuJa's boyfriend)
YuJa	유자	citron tea (PaJeon's girlfriend)
YulMu	율무	'job's tears' tea (YuJa's friend)
PaRam	바람	the wind (slang for a skirt-chaser)
SunSu	선수	an athlete (slang for a player)
Ggachi	까치	the magpie (a bold-breasted chatterbox)
Jaebi	제비	a swallow (also slang for a player)

Disclaimer

All of the characters and situations related herein are fictional and are in no way to be a reflection on any people or actions in real life. Any perceived parallels are merely coincidental, especially as related to ChangHyun.

Hey ChangHyun, *maerrong*. 😎

Rat Ratings

The five rats at the top of each page represent that slang's overall social acceptability. A rating of one would indicate that it is suitable for polite conversation; two rats will be acceptable for some or most informal situations; three crosses over into the realm of the vaguely vulgar (only suitable for close friends and even then, carefully); four rats is considered flat out obscene; and five is so offensive that it's dangerous... you better get ready to fight!

How to use this book

Read it! Study it! Memorize it!
Share it with your friends!
Carry it with you... EVERYWHERE!

How not to use this book

To teach your children English. ("Hey kids, let's practice!")
As a doorstop! (It's far too light.)
To speak to your Korean boss!

A Note on Transliteration

OK, there is old school Idu, Macan-Reishauer, and the new Korean government system (in which Pusan became Busan, and people named Kim and Park are now all supposed to be Gims and Baks)... all of which are lacking in some way. So we adapted our own (loosely speaking), leaning towards the new government system, but sometimes choosing the most natural sounds for English speakers to understand. If you don't like the transliteration, find that it varies between methods, or uses non-traditional methods, too fucking bad – just deal with it. This is not an academic document and we refuse to live by *your* rules.

The Amazingly Mutable Transgender Giuk

Angled for the tongue,

yet guttural and gluttonous for one

       so adept at g's and k's

    though often unsure which. . .

The massively mutable transgender giuk ㄱ;

    It's ㄱㄱㄱ great! — 객객 (gaek, gaek)

간지난다

[gan-ji-nan-da]

to look cool, fierce or snazzy; off the hook

제주도의 방언에서 유래한 것으로 생각된다. 제주도에서는 이 간지라는 단어가 '횃대'를 의미했다. 이 횃대는 옷걸이를 의미하는데 옷태가 잘 나거나, 옷입는 스타일에 감각이 있는 사람을 보고 이 말을 쓴다.(또한 간지는 느낌을 의미하는 일본어로부터 유래되어졌다고 추측되기도 한다.)

Literally "off the rack," but closer to the English slang expression "off the hook." *Ganji* (간지) is Jeju dialectic for *hoidae* (횃대), which means a coat hanger or clothes rack, and is used here to represent a person with a good sense of style as if a voguish sample on a mannequin or a clothes rack. (*Ganji* may also come from the Japanese word for feeling, as in to make a favorable impression.)

간지난 놈

SoYoon	너 간지난다! 오늘 어디 가?
JiYoon	하하 오늘 입사면접이 있어서 신경 좀 썼어.
SoYoon	잠깐만! 그 옷들 어디서 났어?
JiYoon	네 침실 안 옷걸이에 걸려 있었어. 왜, 너 이거 안 입잖아?
SoYoon	내 옷걸이에? 음, 그럼 나도 그 옷 입으면 간지나겠다.
JiYoon	그거는 "off the hook!"이다.

Off the Hook

소윤	Wow, you look ganjinanda. You going somewhere today?
지윤	Ha, ha, my interview's today so I put some effort into it.
소윤	Wait a minute! Where did you get those clothes?
지윤	Off the hook in your bedroom. Why? You weren't using them.
소윤	Off my hook? Well, I guess that makes me ganjinanda too.
지윤	That's "off the hook!"

갈구다

[gal-gu-da]

to tease, nag, irritate or annoy

갈구하다는 것은 본래, 무엇인가를 간절히 바라는 것을 의미한다. 하지만 어찌된건지 현재는 친구들 사이에서, 특정 인물을 심하게 놀리거나 시비거는 행위를 뜻하게 되었다.

Originally meaning a craving, hunger or earnest desire, *galguhada* (갈구하다), it became a slang expression for mocking someone or poking fun at them. It is most often used among friends to get a reaction from (rise out of) them or even to make them angry.

최고의 친구

SeungMan	너 오늘 머리 꼬라지가 왜그러냐? 완전 2:8 가르마네…
DooHwan	와~~?
SeungMan	옷은 또 왜그래? 키 더 작아보여… ㅋㅋ
	어제 소개팅한 애한테도 차였다며~ 하하
DooHwan	아~ 그만 좀 괴롭혀. 맨날 갈궈.
	나만보면 갈구고 지랄이야 짜증나게.

The Best of Friends

승만	What's wrong with your hair today? Perfectly parted 2:8.
두환	Wha~~?
승만	And what's with your clothes? You look shorter… Kh, Kh.
	Your blind date must have kicked you to the curb yesterday. Ha, ha.
두환	Ah, quit mocking me. Everyday, galguda.
	When you see me, galguda. You spaz! You're so annoying.

The Straight Scoop

2:8 [ee-dae-pal] 80% over the top, a combover.

ㅋㅋ [kh-kh] the sound of sniggering.

Blind Date 소개팅 [so-gae-ting] introduction mee-*ting*. See page 84 and 185.

갑이다

[gap-i-da]

born in the same year; a peep or peer

'동갑'이라는 단어가 줄여저, 같은 해에 태어났음을 의미하는 말이다. 특히 한국인들에게는 동갑이면 대체 서로 친구로 지낸다.

Shortened from the Korean *donggap* (동갑), *gabita* describes people born in the same year. Such peers enjoy special relationships (read – instant friendship) in terms of closeness and social equality, which allows them to speak in less formal language to each other.

클럽의 돼지 두마리

ChangHyun 안녕하세요~ 여기 나이트 자주 오세요? 몇년생이세요?

Arum 가끔 와요. 저 83년생이요.

ChangHyun 83년생? 돼지띠? 나도 돼지띠인데. 우리 갑이다.

좋다! 반말하자.

Two Pigs at a Club

창현 Hello, do you come to 'night' (clubs) often?
What year were you born?

아름 I come often. And I was born in 83.

창현 Born in 83? I'm a pig too. We're gapida.
Great! Let's speak banmal.

The Straight Scoop

반말 [ban-mal] to speak comfortably, using low or informal language.

강추

[gang-chu]

it rocks; two thumbs up

'강력추천'이라는 단어의 줄임말로서, 무언가를 강력하게 추천하는 것을 의미한다. 강추는 온라인상 인터넷 채팅에서 종종 사용된다.

Roughly equivalent to the English "it rocks," This expression is an abbreviation of *gangryok chucheon* (강력추천), meaning to strongly recommend something, *gangchu* started online in internet chat rooms by young people, but is now used in everyday conversations. Similar to "It's the shit!"

Antonym: 비추 [bi-chu] not recommended; "it's shit!"

무엇을 볼까...

MinShik	뭘 볼까? 니가 골라.
JiTae	어, 올드보이네... 나 아직 못봤는데.
MinShik	뭐? 아직도 못봤다고? 말도안돼... 꼭봐야지. 강추야 강추.

What to See...

민식	What should we watch? You choose.
지태	Oh, they have *Old Boy*... I haven't seen it yet.
민식	What? You haven't seen it yet? You're kidding ... you have to see it. Gangchuya! It rocks!

Culturally Speaking

The Year of Speaking Plainly

Koreans place a great deal of importance on age in language, dividing people into groups of those older than them (who they must speak to with respectful or formal language ~ *jondaetmal* (존댓말)) and those younger than or the same age as them (who they may speak to with *banmal* (반말)). As such, Koreans have a special affection for someone their own age, sharing a common year in school, a common Chinese zodiac sign, *ddi* (띠), and more.

강남스타일

[gang-nam seu-ta-il]

uptown style; a pretense of affluence; a satire of swank

한국의 슈퍼스타 싸이의 노래제목과 같아 대중화되었다. 강남스타일은 서울의 생기 넘치는 "업타운" 지역에서, 사람들이 입고 행동하는 것에 대한 논평이다. 유명브랜드가게와 비싼 커피숍이 즐비한 "로데오거리"를 자주 다니는 사람들은 그들의 부를 자랑하기 위해 흔히 그들의 외모, 패션, 그리고 과시적인 라이프스타일에 전념한다. 노래는 그들의 치장과 혼란스러운 물질주의 감정에 대한 풍자이다.

Popularized by the Korean superstar, Psy in his hit song, "*Gangnam Style*" is a commentary on how people dress and act on the sassy "uptown" side of Seoul. People that frequent its "Rodeo drive" of name-brand stores and overpriced coffee shops are often focused on external appearances, conspicuous consumption and an ostentatious show of wealth rather than more important things. The song is a satire of their dapper styles and muddled materialistic sensibilities.

원샷과 쇼트 스커트

Psy   근혜씨, 축하해! 방금 당선됐어! 이제 뭘 할거야?

GeunHye   우선, 이 $12짜리 커피 마시고 로데오에 가서 프라다 좀 사려고…

Psy   아싸! 원샷! 그게 진정한 강남스타일! 그리고 나서는?

GeunHye   그리고 나서 "강남스타일"을 금지할거야!

Psy   뭐?! 내 노래를? 나의 이 기막힌 춤을? 내 간지스타일?

GeunHye   아니지, 오빠. 난 오빠 노래 무지 좋아해, 그게 아니라 fashion police 불렀다고! 짧은 치마 입은 애들 다 잡아야지!

Psy   안돼~~~

          그건 내가 제일 좋아하는 거라고! 그건 아주 강남답지 못해!

One Shot and Too Short

싸이 GeunHye shi, Congrats! You just got elected!
What will you do next?

근혜 First, I'm going to throw back this $12 coffee and head to Rodeo to buy some Prada....

싸이 Ah-SA! One Shot! That's very Gangnam Style of you! And then?

근혜 I'm going to ban "Gangnam Style!"

싸이 What?! Ban my song? My super fabulous dance?
My ganji style?

끈혜 No, Oppa. I love your song, but I've called out the fashion police! Those short skirts have got to go!

싸이 Noooooo, that's my favorite part! That's not very Gangnam of you!

개기다

[gae-gi-da]

to rebel or be defiant; get sassy; trippin'

본래 닳거나 해지다, 성가시게 달라붙다라는 의미를 가지고 있는 '개개다'라는 단어로부터 변형된 말. 여기서는 자신보다 힘이 센, 더 높은 위치에 있는 사람에게 대들거나 반항하는 모습을 이르는 말로 설명하고자 한다.

From the original *gaegaeda* (개개다), to wear out clothes or to rub the wrong way, as with annoying someone by tagging along, this changed to *gaegida* with the meaning of picking a fight (used when a weaker person talks back to a stronger one) as if an act of rebelling against one's master. Similar to "get smart with" or "sass" someone.

Also: 하극상 [ha-gug-sang] defy an order (in the army); mutiny

불쌍한 참새

Batman	로빈아! 매점가서 컵라면 사와!
Robin	귀찮아. 넌 손이 없어? 발이 없어? 네가 직접 사먹어.
Batman	개기는거야? 그렇게 개기다가 한대 맞는다.
Robin	나 때리면, 다음 시험 때 누구 시험지 베끼려고 그래?

Poor Sparrow

배트맨	Robin-a. Go get me a *cup-ramyon* from the school store.
로빈	How annoying. You don't have hands? No feet? You go buy it and eat it yourself.
배트맨	You gaegida me? If you gaegida like this, I'll smack you.
로빈	If you hit me, whose test will you copy off of next time?

The Straight Scoop

To call someone **neoiga** (네가) is the lowest form of 'you' and would be offensive to someone older.

The '-a' (아), -ya (–야) or -i (–이) **ending on a name** is a diminutive of familiarity similar to the French -ette.

Culturally Speaking

Yakety, Yak. Don't Talk Back

Establishing hierarchy in even relationships is common in Korea as strict hierarchical systems and Confucian values are the norm. This is often true even among peers within the same group with some member establishing themselves as the leader or alpha and expecting others to do their bidding. At times this can resemble a mafia-like structure and is often associated with bullying in school .

개드립

[gae-deu-lib]

give up on the ad-lib; NOT funny

문자 그대로, 개 (무언가 아주 나쁜 것을 의미 – 영어의 bitch와 유사)와 에드립의 합성어. 이 표현은 누군가 재미없는 사람에게 사용된다.

Literally, *gae* or dog (meaning something really bad – related to the English "bitch," but think "dog-tired") combined with *ad-lib* (or improvising), this expression is used to tell someone that they are so NOT funny, to give it up or to just get over themselves.

2007 개드립에서 2012 쥐드립까지

MyungBak	악, 정희… 소식 들었어? 네 딸이 나한테 덤비고 있어.
	무덤 속에서 탄식하고 있겠네. 내가 기가 막혀서!
ChungHee	명박아, 명박아, 내 딸은 분명히 널 꺾고 말거야!
MyungBak	하! 그거 재미있네, 웃겨 진짜! 야 개드립 떨지마! 여자 대통령! 허!
ChungHee	그리고 네 나이 반도 되지 않는 북한 독재자는 널 약해 보이게 할거야!
MyungBak	개드립 더 떨어봐! 말도 안 되는 소리!

2007 Gaedeulib to 2012 Chuidelib

명박	Ach, ChungHee… did you hear? Your daughter is running against me. I'll bet you're turning over in your grave. How absurd!
정희	MyungBak-ah, MyungBak-ah, my daughter will succeed you!
명박	Ha! That's soooo funny, NOT! Stop gaedeulibing me! A woman president! Huh!
정희	And a North Korean dictator less than half your age will make you look weak!
명박	More gaedelib! Preposterous!

겁나게

[geop-na-gae]

hella; (menacingly) much

겁나게의 본래 의미는 무섭거나 두려운 것을 의미한다. 하지만 전라도와 충청남도의 사투리에서는 두려울 만큼 많은 양을 의미하여 엄청, 매우의 의미로 사용되어진다.

Geopnagae's original meaning is "to be scared," but in the Jeollado and South Chungchungdo dialects, it is used to mean very much, or literally, as much as a good scare. Similar to the English intensifiers "heaps" or "wicked." Also, *geopna* (겁나) for short.

겨울의 날씨

Peter	날씨가 왜이래? 일주일 내내 영하 20도야!
SiWoo	응, 밖에 겁나게 추워.
Peter	추운걸 무서워한다고?
SiWoo	아니 바보야, 겁나게는 남쪽 사투리로 좆나게 춥다는 말이야!

Wintry Weather

피터	What's with the weather? It's been 20 degrees below for a week!
시우	Yeah, it's gopnagae cold out there.
피터	You're scared of the cold?
시우	No silly, gopnagae is southern dialect for really fucking cold!

The Straight Scoop

좆나게 [jot na gae] very or much. Similar to the English intensifier "fucking," it literally means for a penis to get hard or "come out."

고고씽

[go-go-ssing]

get a move on; get crackin'; let's went

씽은, 빠른 자동차를 묘사하는 의성어 씽씽으로부터 유래하였다. 이것이 영어 단어 go를 두 번 반복한 것과 결합되어 친구에게 무언가를 재촉하는 경우에 쓰이고있다.

Ssing comes from the Korean *ssing ssing* (씽씽), an onomatopoeic word to describe a speeding vehicle. This is combined with the English word "go," repeated twice, to urge friends to speed. Mainly used on the internet and in text messaging to relate the need for speed and somewhat similar to "go go go," "we've got to hustle," "pick up the pace," or "let's haul ass!"

기말고사

WonDong 드디어 시험이 끝났구나! 넌 뭐할거야?

DongWon 술이나 빨러 고고씽해야지. 같이 가자!

WonDong 그래, 넌 답을 알고 있었어. 그럼 넌 A받는거야.

 A는 'Alcohol'이라는 뜻이지. 고고씽하자!

Finals

원동 Finally, the test is over! What do you want to do?

동원 I'd better gogossing to suck down a drink.

 Let's go together.

원동 Ah, you knew the answer. You get an 'A' for Alcohol.

 Let's gogossing!

The Straight Scoop

빨러 [bbal-leo] literally "to lick or to suck down." This slang used often among young people for drinking alcohol, smoking up, or taking drugs (getting high).

고딩 (초딩, 중딩, 대딩, 직딩)

[go-ding (cho-ding, jung-ding, dae-ding, jik-ding)]

a high schooler
(elementary, middle school, university student, office worker)

청소년들이 문자메시지나 온라인 상에서 고등학생이라는 단어를 줄여 만든 말.

Short for *godeunghaksaeng* (고등학생), this expression is primarily used among young people for texting or online chatting. Combining the "*d*" (ㄷ) with the "*ng*" (ㅇ) of *deung-hak-sang* (등학생) to make "*ding*" (딩) and appending that to the initial character of the level of student or worker: e.g. *go* (고) for *godeunghakyo* (고등학교).

채팅방

HaPum	나 어제 채팅방에서 귀여운 남자 만났어.
HanSum	나이 많아?
HaPum	아니, 걔 고딩이야. 그런데 걔 만나봤는데 담배 피더라....
HanSum	그래서?
HaPum	난 담배피는 고딩들 싫어!
HanSum	담배피는 대딩들은?
HaPum	걔네는 완전 멋있지!

The Chat Room

하품	I met a cute guy in the chat room yesterday.
한숨	Is he older?
하품	No, he's a goding. But then I met him and found out that he smokes....
한숨	So what?
하품	I don't like godings that smoke!
한숨	What about daedings that smoke?
하품	They're so cool!

고춧가루 뿌리다

[go-chu-ga-ru bbu-ri-da]

to ruin (a situation); to be a party pooper

고춧가루를 뿌리는 것은 무엇인가를 맵게, 입에 맞지 않게 만드는 것을 의미한다. 바꾸어 말하면, 상황을 망치는 것인데, 특별히 누군가가 이성을 만날 때 쓰이는 표현이다. "다 된 밥에 재 뿌리다"와 비슷한 의미로 누군가의 단점에 대해 말하는 것이다.

Literally "to sprinkle red pepper," *gochugaru bburida* means to make something too spicy or even unpalatable. In other words, to ruin a situation, especially when trying to meet someone of the opposite sex. Akin to "다 된 밥에 재 뿌리다" (*da doen babae jae burinda*) – literally, sprinkling ashes on cooked rice, meaning to talk about someone's bad points (or messing up at the end). Similar English expressions: "throw a wet blanket on something," "be a killjoy," or even "to cock-block someone."

여장실

ChangHyun	나영아, 무슨 일이야? 나랑 소개팅하던 사람 어디 갔어?
SoYoon	오, 너가 화장실 갔을 때 태용이가 지난 주말에 대해 이야기했어.
ChangHyun	뭐?! 여자한테 그 얘기를 했어? 넌 왜 맨날 고춧가루 뿌려.
TaeYong	그냥 완전 재밌자나! – 너가 여장실에 들어가서 완전 처음보는 여자랑 키스하고 껴안고 난리친거. 너 엄청 취했었잖아!

The Girls' Room

창현	SoYoon, what happened? Where did my date go?
소윤	Oh, when you were in the bathroom, TaeYong talked about last weekend.
창현	What?! You told her the story? Why do you always gochugaru bburida.
태용	It's just so funny! – You walking in the girls' room, makin' out with a complete stranger. You were so drunk!

The Straight Scoop

여장실 [yeo-jang-shil] the girl's (bath)room, short for 여자화장실.

골때린다

[gol-ddae-rin-da]

to be a buffoon or play the part of the fool

글자 그대로, 뇌를 때린다는의미. 누군가 멍청한 짓, 혹은 이상한 행동을 하여 어떻게 반응을 해야할지 모를 때, 골때린다고 한다. 유사한 영어표현: "어딘가 머리를 박은게 분명해!"

Literally, to hit the brain. When someone does something stupid or acts weird and you don't know how to react, you would say "*golddaerinda.*" Similar to the English: "He must have been dropped on his head!" or "What a noob!"

Also: 빵꾸똥꾸 [bbang-gu-ddong-gu] childish for fool, literally "fart-poop."

패션 폴리스

JiYoon	나 너무 추워.
HeeYeon	그런데 왜 이 한겨울에 스커트를 입고 짧은 소매 셔츠를 입었어?
JiYoon	멋있게 보이고 싶어서.
HeeYeon	너 진짜 골때린다!
	나는 fashion police가 너를 체포하길 바래.

Fashion Police

지윤	I'm so cold.
회연	Well, then why did you wear a skirt and short-sleeved shirt in the middle of winter?
지윤	I want to look good.
회연	You are so golddaerinda!
	I hope you get arrested by the fashion police.

The Straight Scoop

Fashion Police는 가상의 그룹으로 이상한 옷을 입는 사람을 저지하는 사람들을 의미.

A made-up group who stop people from committing fashion faux pas.

골초 or 꼴초

[gol-cho]

a chain smoker or tobacco fiend

본래는 품질이 나쁜 담배를 의미하였는데, 현재는 담배를 많이 피우는 사람을 이르는 말이 되었다. (담배를 많이 피우는 사람들은 그들의 많은 양의 담배를 사기위해 값이 싼 것을 사야만 했다고 추측된다.) 유사한 영어표현으로는 "굴뚝처럼 담배피다"라는 표현이 있다.

Originally meaning low quality tobacco, *golcho* has come to refer to someone who smokes heavily. (Presumably they must smoke cheap tobacco to afford their habit.) Related to the English "chain smoker" or "smokes like a chimney."

Other smoking slang: 아리까다 [ya-ri-gga-da] to smoke (on the sly)

흡연의 고마움

Bom	여보, 당신한테 골초냄새 난다. 내가 없는 동안 담배 시작했어?
KaEul	아니요, 단지 "완전 즐거운" 저녁 회식이 있었어요.
	담배 안 피는 사람은 나밖에 없었구요.
Bom	그래, 그럼 일단 그 냄새나는 옷부터 벗고 ~우~ 그 골초냄새
	없애려면 내가 좀 씻겨줘야겠어.

Thank You for Smoking

봄	Honey, you smell like a golcho.
	Did you start smoking while I was away?
가을	No, I just had a "wonderful" evening meeting with
	my coworkers. I must be the only one that doesn't smoke.
봄	Well, then let's get you out of those smelly clothes and ~oooh~
	scrub you down to get rid of that golcho smell.

24

공주병

[gong-ju-byeong]

little princess syndrome; snob; self-entitled bitch

공주라는 단어와 병이라는 단어가 결합되어 만들어진 말. 실제로 공주병이라는 병은 존재하지 않지만, 젊은 여성이 마치 자기 자신이 공주처럼 예쁘다고 착각하는 것을 보고 공주병에 걸렸다고 한다. 이와 관련있는 영어표현으로는 신데렐라 콤플렉스나 JAP가 있다.

Literally, a combination of princess and disease, *gongjubeong* describes a woman with the illusion that she is a princess and therefore should be treated like one. Related to the English "Cinderella Complex" or "JAP" (Jewish American Princess), yet these American equivalents also imply aspects of money and privilege that the Korean does not.

Also: 보슬아치 [bo-seul-a-chi] a self important bitch.

난 너무 예뻐

MinHee	희연아! 이거 오늘 새로 산 옷인데 어때?
	나 너무 예뻐진 것 같지 않아?
HeeYeon	아, 공주병 너무 심하다!
MinHee	"아임 소우 프리티. 오우 소우 프리티."
HeeYeon	알았어, 너 죽~인다. 죽여. 그냥 죽어라!

I'm so Pretty

민희	How do you like my new dress, HeeYeon?
	Doesn't it make me look beautiful?
희연	Ah, too much of a gongjubyeong!
민희	"I'm so pretty. Oh so pretty."
희연	OK, you're to die for ... to die for. Then die!

The Straight Scoop

죽인다 [juk-in-da] **to die for.** Literally "I will kill you," this is a commonly used expression meaning wonderful or great, or in this case: hot, and though related to 죽을래 [juk-ul-lae] **you wanna die,** it does not have the same connotation.

구라까다

[gu-ra-gga-da]

to bullshit someone; to front

구라는 거짓(말)이나 가짜, 이야기를 속되게 이르는 말을 의미한다. 그리고 이것은 까다 (알이 부화하는 것)와 치다(때리다 또는 저지르다)라는 동사와 함께 결합되어 사용되어진 다. 단순히 거짓말 하는 것을 의미하거나 축어적으로는 거짓말을 알이 부화하듯 계속 깐 다, 거짓말을 하고 이야기를 지어내는 행위를 의미한다.

Gura (a lie or a vulgar way of telling dirty jokes) is combined with *ggada* (as in to hatch an egg) or *chida* (to strike or to commit) to mean simply to lie or more literally, hatch a lie, commit a lie, or just get fictitious.

돌 둘

JungSeok 난 창현이가 좋아. 맨날 말을 지어내는게 문제지.

HwaSeok 맞아, 항상 구라까…

 걔가 할 줄 아는건 구라까는 것 밖에 없어.

JungSeok 하지만 걔 정말 웃겨. 야, 우리 걔한테 구라쳐보자.

HwaSeok 그래, 터무니 없는 거짓말해서 걔가 얼마나 좋아하는지 한번 보자구.

JungSeok "불은 불로 다스린다"

Two Rocks

정석 I like ChangHyun, but he's always making things up.

화석 Yeah, every day guraggada … all he does, nothing but guraggada.

정석 But he's so funny. Ya, let's gurachida to him.

화석 Yeah, a whopper of a lie and see how he likes it.

정석 Fight fire with fire!

구리다

[gu-ri-da]

to be foul, disgusting or ghastly; lack taste

본래, 똥이나 방귀 냄새와 같이 지독한 냄새를 의미하는 말. 요즘은 젊은 사람들 사이에서 어떤것의 외향이나 행태가 좋지 않을 때 쓰이고 있다.

Originally meaning the smell of dung or methane gas, *gurida* is used among young people for someone or something that looks and acts poorly, smelly, somewhat shady or even fishy. Similar to the British "dreadful" or "ghastly," or the American expressions "that is so foul," "so gross!" or just plain "godawful!"

소개팅

HeeYeon   어제 만난 남자 어땠어?

MinHee   아, 완전 구렸어... 옷 입는 것도 구리고, 자기 잘난척만 하고.

그 남자 다시는 보기 싫어. 아무튼 최악이었어.

HeeYeon   그럼... 내가 꼬셔볼까?

Blind Date

희연   How was the guy you met yesterday?

민희   Ah, absolutely gurida.... His style was gurida, and he only bragged about himself. I never want to see him again. Anyway, it was terrible.

희연   Well, then... can I try?

Some Ghastly Synonyms

From Glib to Grim to Glaringly Gross

후지다 [hu-ji-da] lousy; inferior; a lemon.

꼬지다 [ggo-ji-da] out of fashion; dated; passé.

좆같다 [jot-cat-da] like shit (lit. like a dick).

귀차니즘

[gui-cha-nism]

the couch potato principle; a tiresome existence

귀찮다와 ~ism이 결합되어 귀찮고 성가신것을 찾는 주의를 뜻하게 되었다. 젊은이들은 모든것을 귀찮아하며 불평하고, 그래서 아무것도 하기싫어하는 그들의 게으른 친구들을 묘사하기 위해 이 신조어를 만들어냈다.

Part of the "can't be bothered" movement and the "sick and tired" masses with the addition of an ~ism to *guichanta*, which means to find things bothersome. Young people coined this word to describe their lazy friends, who fall into the habit of complaining about being tired or *guichanta* so they don't want to do anything.

Also: 귀차니스트 [gui-cha-nist] someone who has fallen into *guichanism*.

오타쿠 [o-ta-ku] a stay-at-home, antisocial, animae-watching, game-playing geek or nerd that is so obsessed with something that they cannot form proper relationships (from the Japanese for house).

귀찮아!

Peter   창현이는 왜 안불렀어?

SiWoo   초대했는데 요즘 그 자식 귀차니즘에 빠져서 숨 쉬는 것 조차도 귀찮대.

Peter   아 맞다, 걔 가끔 귀차니스트 같지~

Can't be Bothered!

피터   Why didn't you call ChangHyun?

시우   I invited him, but these days that little brat fell into guichanism.
Since then, he says that even breathing is tiresome.

피터   Yeah, sometimes he's such a guichanist!

까리하다

[gga-ri-ha-da]

to look cool, pimped, pimpin'

멋있는 사람을 보고하는 말. 길거리를 떠도는 사람을 속되게 일컫던 말 '까리'라는 말에서 지금의 긍정적인 의미로 변화된 것으로 보인다.

반의어: 추하다와 구리다가 합쳐진 추리하다가 있다.

Literally meaning street-walker, scoundrel or vagrant, *ggarihada* has come to mean stylish or *meoshita* (멋있다) in Korean similar to the changes in the meaning of "bad" or "pimped" in English.

Antonym: 추리하다 [chu-ri-ha-da] looks bad or homely, from *chuhada* (추하다) mixed with *gurida* (구리다)

옷 사냥꾼들

PaJeon	저사람 봐! 진짜 까리하다.
YuJa	다 옷빨이야. 그거 빼고는 추리해. 자기가 훨씬 멋져.
PaJeon	고맙다 내사랑.
YuJa	이제, 너한텐 저 사람 옷만 있으면 돼... 저놈 잡으러 가자!

Clothes Hunters

파전	Oh, look at that guy! He's really ggarihada.
유자	Only his clothes, other than that he's churihae. You look much better, honey.
파전	Thanks my love.
유자	Now, you just need his clothes... let's get him!

The Straight Scoop

옷빨이야 [eot-bbal-i-ya] literally, only his clothes. This implies that though his style is great, his other attributes are lacking – in other words, he's fugly.

까다

[gga-da]

to scrape knuckles; to beat, thrash or pound someone

누군가를 때리는 행위를 속되게 이르는 말. 본래의 의미 "까다"는 껍질 따위를 벗긴다는
의미인데, 상대방을 치거나 때려 살 껍질을 벗겨내겠다는 의미를 함축하고 있다.

Ggada's original meaning is to peel (as in an apple or orange) and has inspired many
idioms and slang expressions. Here, it refers to beating someone, as the skin of the
knuckles will be bruised or scraped off. Some English equivalents would be to
scrap, brawl or rumble; also to "give someone a beat-down" or to "throw down."
Ggada can also mean to speak ill of someone or to turn someone down.

남자는 남자답게 산다

KwangSung   화석! 너 어제 얻어터졌다며? 누구한테 맞은거야?

HwaSeok   체대 다니는 애.

KwangSung   체대? 체대라고 해봐야 별거 아니야. 내가 까줄게.

[다음날...]

HwaSeok   광성! 얼굴이 왜 그래? 멍이 시퍼렇게 들었네.

KwangSung   미안해 화석아. 체대 놈은 역시 다르긴 다르더라.
            까러 갔다가 되려 엄청 까였어!

The Straight Scoop

되려 [doi-ryeo] is provincial dialectic for *do-ri-o* (도리어), the Korean word for "on
the contrary," though it can be heard in Seoul as well.

Boys will be Boys

광성   HwaSeok! I heard you got punched yesterday. Who hit you?

화석   A physical education student.

광성   Physical education? Physical education is nothing.
I'll go ggada for you.

[The next day....]

화석   KwangSung! What happened to your face?
You're all black and blue.

광성   Sorry, HwaSeok. Those physical education bastards are truly
different – yeah, they're different. I went to ggada, but quite the
opposite got ggada-ed.

Culturally Speaking

A 'Physical' Education

Someone majoring in physical education (체대 다니는 애) in Korea is treated differently by both the school and other students. They often act like a kind of mafia in their use of respectful language and their interactions with others in their major. Describing someone as *Choidae* would be somewhat like describing them as "a rugby player" or "a football player," but would also have some element of menace due to the solidarity of the group. *Choidae* students are often treated with deference at the school, given fewer requirements and held to lower standards in class.

깔(따구)

[ggal(dda-gu)]

a girlfriend; (someone's) bitch

1990년대에 청소년들에 의해 사용되어지기 시작했다. 깔따구는 각다귀라는 단어에서 변형되어졌다. 각다귀는 통속적으로 줄무늬 모기, 기생충 또는 흡혈귀를 의미한다. 이와같이, 이 단어는 부정적 의미를 함축하고 있다. 아마도 이 단어는 한국사람들이 데이트를 할 때 남자들이 주로 돈을 쓰는 것에서 유래한 것 같다. 젠장!

Started in the 1990's by teenagers, *ggalddagu* comes from the word *gagdagui* (각다귀), literally meaning a stripped mosquito, and referring to a parasite or a blood-sucking girlfriend. As such, it has a negative connotation, possibly in reference to the fact that when Koreans date, the man is almost always expected to pay for everything. Damn!

남자의 세상?

KwangSung	병식이 요새 안보이네?
HwaSeok	그 새끼 깔 생겼어.
KwangSung	아~ 깔따구 생겨서 요즘 잠수타는거구나.
HwaSeok	응. 걔 우리랑 놀 돈도 없을걸?
KwangSung	그래. 그 깔 때문에 우린 친구 한 명을 또 잃었어.
HwaSeok	이제 우리 둘만 남았네? 우린 서로 배신하지 말자…
KwangSung	그래, "하나를 위한 둘 그리고 모두를 위한 하나."

A Man's World?

광성	Haven't seen Byungshik lately?
화석	That SOB got a ggal.
광성	Ah~ got a ggalddagu…. That's why he's submerged these days.
화석	Eung. Even if he's not with her, he's got no money left to hang out with us.
광성	Yep, because of that ggal, we lost another friend.
화석	Now we only have each other left. Let's not betray each other….
광성	Yeah, "Two for one and one for all."

Sound Box I

What Sounds Like Onomatopoeia?

The Korean language is rich with onomatopoeia or *eui-seong-eo* (의성어) and other expressive sound words. Below are just a few.

- **아야** [a-ya] Ouch!
- **앗** [at] Oops!
- **음** [mm] Um...
- **응** [eung] similar to the English "yeah."
- **으** [eu] a true lazyman's "yes." Also – **어** [oh], **엉** [eong], **아** [ah].
- **우와** [woo-ah] an expression of awe and surprise, similar to "wow!"
- **에이** [ae-i] an expression of disbelief.
- **으이구** [eu-i-gu] poor you. Equivalent to the Korean expression *igo* (**아이고**). *Igo*, meaning "oh my," "good gracious" or "woe is me," would be used as a type of sigh or expression of frustration or surprise to oneself. The *euigu*, however, would be used for another person (not oneself) as with the English "poor baby."
- **흥!** [heung] or **치!** [chi] (or some combination thereof) a snarky expression for when a Korean girl sulks to her boyfriend.
- **딸랑딸랑** [ddal-rang-ddal-rang] the sound of a bell on a dog's collar used to represent a kiss ass or someone who sucks up to a boss.
- **휴** [hyu] equivalent to the American "whew" (used to express relief).
- **냠냠** [nyam-nyam] a sound made when chewing food.
- **칙칙폭폭** [chik-chik-pok-pok] chugga chugga choo choo train sound.
- **쾅** [kwang] a crashing sound.
- **빵** [bbang] Bang!

33

꺄 or 꺅

[kkya] or [kkyak]

LOL; "Oh, joy!"

꺄는 단순한 기쁨의 감탄사이다! 보통 "~~~"를 끝에 붙이며, 문자메시지나 카카오톡에서 많이 사용된다: 꺄~~~는 일반적으로 여성이 많이 사용하지만, 귀엽게 행동하고 싶은 남자들(보통 게이라고 함)도 많이 쓴다.

Kkya is simply an onomatopoeic exclamation of joy! Often including an "~~~" ending, and most often used in text messaging or on KakaoTalk: *Kkya ~~~* is used by and large by females to describe shrieks of joy, but can be used by men who want to act cute (read – gay) as well.

꺄톡

JiYoon	언니이이이, 그거 알아?
SoYoon	뭐?
JiYoon	나 새 옷 생겼어! 꺄~
SoYoon	음
JiYoon	그리고 언니이이이, 이거 어디 것인 줄 알아?
SoYoon	…어, 어디…?
JiYoon	프라다!!! 꺄~~ 그리고 언니이이이, 어디서 났게?
SoYoon	;;; 어디서 났는데…
JiYoon	남자친구가 사줬어. 꺄~~~~
SoYoon	헐…

KkyaTalk

지윤	Onni-i-i-i, guess what?
소윤	What?
지윤	I got a new dress! Kkya~
소윤	Mmm.
지윤	And onni-i-i-i, guess where I got it from?
소윤	…uh, where…?
지윤	PRADA!!! Kkya~~ And Onni-i-i-i, guess how I got it?
소윤	;;; how…
지윤	From my new boyfriend. Kkya~~~
소윤	Heol…

34

깝치다

[ggap-chi-da]

to fool around, clown around or goof off

까불다, 깝죽거리다와 비슷한 의미로 경망스럽고 방정맞은 행위를 이르는 말. 일제 강점기에 쓰여진 이상화 시인의 봄에 관한 시, '빼앗긴 들에도 봄은 오는가'에서도 다루어진 표현이다.

Similar to *gabulda* (까불다) or *gapjukgorita* (깝죽거리다) and meaning to behave flippantly or act rashly, this was coined by the poet *Lee SangHwa* (이상화) in a poem about spring, called "*bbaeatgil deulaedo bomeun oneunga*" (빼앗긴 들에도 봄은 오는가) during the Japanese occupation – described here.

나비와 제비

ChangHyun	시우야 저 계집애 어때? 번호나 따올까?
SiWoo	"나비 제비야 깝치지 마라 / 맨드라미 들마꽃에도 인사를 해야지"
ChangHyun	뭐라고? 또 미친 시적인 소리 하고 있네!
SiWoo	알았어, 내가 쉽게 말해줄게. 깝치지 말고 다시 들어가서 공부나 하자.

The Swallow and the Butterfly

창현	Hey SiWoo, how about that chick? Should I get her number?
시우	"Hey butterfly, hey swallow, don't ggapchida. You have to say hello to the cockscomb in the field."
창현	What did you say? Again with the crazy poetry talk!
시우	All right, I'll put it to you in plain words…. Instead of ggapchida, let's go back in and study.

The Straight Scoop

KkyaTalk refers to KakaoTalk, the Korean smartphone, free messenger app equivalent to WhatsApp.

;;; – a way of texting that you are annoyed with someone.

헐 [heol] OMG; oops; tisk; whatever. See page 228 for more information.

깡(다구)

[ggang(da-gu)]

steeled for action; having balls (of steel)

깡이 세다, 깡이 있다라는 표현으로 많이 쓰이며, 이 "깡"은 지기 싫어하는 악착같은 오기를 의미한다. "깡"은 북한에서 강철을 의미하고, "다구"는 맷돌을 의미하는데, 강철과 맷돌같이 센 성격을 가지고 있다하여 이와같이 변형된 것으로 추측된다.

Coming from the expression *ggangi saeda* (깡이 세다), which actually originates from the North Korean word *ggang* (깡) for steel, and the *-dagu* (다구) ending, which comes from the Korean word for millstone. Overall, this is suggestive of someone that has courage, nerve, an unyielding spirit or is simply reluctant to admit defeat.

멍청한 깡다구

ChangHyun   겁쟁이. 깡다구도 없냐? 평일날 무슨 음주단속이야.

ByungShik   아~ 몰라 난 깡이 없어서 운전 못하겠어?

              깡다구 센 네가 운전해!

ChangHyun   알았어. 이 겁쟁이야. 내가 할게.

              〔10분 후...〕

Police Officer 음주단속이 있겠습니다. "후"하고 힘차게 불어주십쇼.

ChangHyun   제발 한번만 봐주세요. 이제부터 안할게요.

ByungShik   ㅋㅋㅋ 깡다구 세다더니 꼴 좋다.

Drunken Decisions

창현
Coward. Don't you have any ggangdagu?

On a weekday would there be a sobriety check?

병식
Ah~ I don't know. I don't have any ggang so I can't drive. You have the strong ggangdagu, so you drive!

창현
OK. You coward. I'll do it.

[10 minutes later...]

경찰
Sobriety check, sir. Blow into the device.

창현
Please look at me nicely one time. I won't do it any more.

병식
Kh Kh Kh. Your ggangdagu is strong all right...
looking good.

The Straight Scoop

한번만 봐주세요 [han-beon-man bua-ju-sae-yo] would be literally translated as look at me (nicely) one time. It is a common request to ask for forgiveness or for the person to turn a blind eye to your misdeed.

(확)깬다

[(hoak)ggaen-da]

to break a trance; shatter an image; be over it

상대방이 어처구니없는 말이나 행동을 할 때 창피를 주기위해 쓰는 말. "깬다"라는 단어는 본래 술이 깨다, 잠에서 깨다 등의 표현에 사용되는데 여기서는 상대방의 엉뚱한 행동으로 인해 술이나 잠에서 깨어날 정도로 황당하고 부끄러운것의 의미를 내포한다.

Ggaenda (깬다) literally means "to break," from *ggaeda* (깨다), and relates to *cham ggaenda* (잠 깬다) and *sul ggaenda* (술 깬다) meaning to suddenly rouse from sleep or to sober up. Here, it is to say that some impression or spell has been broken by another's absurd or shameful action. Similar to the English expressions "for shame," "my image of you is shot," or essentially to be "over someone."

짝사랑 1

Arum	희연아, 저기좀 봐, 네 꿈의 이상형이 간다.
	오, 저 남자 멋쟁이이고 너무 잘생겼어.
HeeYeon	태용? 어디? 완전 조각상이야.
	언젠가는 저 남자랑 결혼하고 말테야...
HeeYeon	이럴수가, 확 깬다.
Arum	왜? 무슨 일이야?
HeeYeon	저것 봐! 저 남자 자기 코 파고 있어! 아 이젠 끝이야.
	정말 깬다.

Unrequited Love 1

아름	HeeYeon-a, look over there. There goes the man of your dreams. Oh, he's such a sharp dresser and so handsome.
회연	TaeYong? Where? Oh, he's like a sculpture! I'll marry him someday...
회연	Oh no, hoak ggaenda.
아름	Why? What happened?
회연	Look! He's picking his nose! I'm so over him. Totally ggaenda.

38

Culturally Speaking

"Hello Cutie"

Being overly cute, or at least acting cute, *gui-yeo-un chok* [귀여운 척], (think Hello Kitty) remains part of the game for many Korean women well beyond their teens. While often used as a pretense, it is also thought of as a sign of innocence and purity. Such girls will add lots of cute expressions, icons, hearts, etc. to their conversations to convey their sweetness and use *egyo* [애교] (acting with intense childish cuteness and affectionate mannerisms) toward their male counterparts, to cajole or coerce them to get something they want. If someone takes this to an extreme, you can call them on it by saying *guichok hajima* [귀척 하지마] – give up on the excessive cuteness.

꺼져

[ggeo-jeo]

get out; take a hike; piss off; bite me

"꺼져"라는 표현은 영어의 "Go away!" "Get out of my sight!"와 같이 여기서 나가라는 의미의 말이다. 하지만 속어로 쓰일 때에는 "난 널 믿을 수 없어!", "싫어!"의 의미를 포함하고 있다.

Literally meaning "go away" or "get out of my sight," but when used as slang, *ggeojeo* can mean "I don't believe you," or "I don't want to." Similar to the English expressions "get out," "no way," "not going to happen" or even "fuck off!"

찬 물

Ggachi	야, 오늘 클럽데인데 홍대갈래?
Jaebi	좋지, 그런데 꼭 M2위에 있는 클럽 가야해.
Ggachi	꺼져! 너 그 소영이란 여자가 오길 바라는 거자나.
Jaebi	응, 걔 진짜 예쁘고 어려. ㅋㅋ.
Ggachi	꺼져! 걔는 아줌마야!! 그 여자 서른살도 넘었어.
Jaebi	아마 그럼 난 늙은 여자를 좋아하나봐. 암튼 찬 물 끼얹지마 이새끼야.

Cold Water

까치	Hey man, want to go to Hongdae for club night?
제비	Sure, but we absolutely have to go to that club above M2.
까치	Ggeojyeo! You're just hoping that SoYoung will be there.
제비	Yeah, but she is so beautiful and *so young*. Kh, Kh.
까치	Ggeojyeo! She's an ajumma!! She's got to be over thirty.
제비	Maybe I like older women then. Don't throw cold water on it, you SOB.

The Straight Scoop

아줌마 [a-jum-ma] literally "a married woman," but most often used to refer to an older-looking, short, stocky matron with short hair in a bad perm (think – old bag). As such, most women would not like to be called an 'ajumma,' even if married.

꽝이다

[gwang-i-da]

to come up empty; zilch; all for nothing

축어적 의미 – 아무것도 아니다. "꽝"은 보통 망치를 두드리는 것과 같은 무엇인가에 충격을 주는 소리(꽝꽝)이지만, 이 표현에서는 바라던 무엇인가의 부재를 의미한다.

Literally "it's nothing." *Gwang* is normally a percussive sound (꽝꽝~ *gwang gwang*) like the banging of a hammer, but here it means the absence of something – usually, something wished for or narrowly missed, as with a losing lottery ticket.

당첨자와 비당첨자

ByungShik	와우, 나 10캔 당첨이야 ~ 너 것도 봐봐.
	뚜껑에 뭐라고 나왔는지.
KwangSung	에이. "다음기회를 이용해 주세요." 꽝이다…
	내가 하는건 전부 꽝이야. ㅉㅉ.

Winners and Losers

병식	Wow, I won a 10 can prize ~ Take a look!
	Take a look at yours and see what you got.
광성	Ay-e. "Please try again." Gwangida….
	all I ever get is gwang. Ts ts.

Sound Box II

The Sweet Sound of a Snigger

ㅉㅉ [jj-jj] or [ts ts] similar to a tisk tisk sound, this sound means "too bad."

ㅋㅋ [kh-kh] the sound of sniggering, ㅎㅎ [he-he] short for laughter.

ㄷㄷ [deu-deu] from 후덜덜 [hu-deol-deol] make me shiver (when scared or cold)

쿄쿄 [kyo-kyou] cute giggling, 캬캬 [kya-kya-kya] evil laugh, snigger

음훼훼훼 [eum-hwe-hwe-hwe] sinister laughter or a guffaw when victorious

푸하하 [pu-ha-ha] for actual laughter, (ㅋㅋ or ㅎㅎ are most often used to
      lighten the mood of a conversation rather than indicate real laughter)

꼬라지

[ggo-ra-ji]

to be homely, odd or unsightly

꼴이란 상태, 모양을 뜻하는 단어에서 변형된 말. 옷입는 것, 춤추는 것, 외모나 스타일 등을 보고 주로 부정적인 의미로 사용된다.

Coming from the word *ggol* (꼴), which means a shape, state of being, a look or a plight, this expression is usually used to describe clothing, dancing, a look or style, etc. (rather than a person) as having a homely appearance or unsightly form.

홍대의 클럽 데이

PaRam   너 방금 걸어간 계집애 봤어? 정말 죽인다!

SunSu   죽인다고? 창녀 같아. 어떻게 저런 꼬라지로

옷을 입을 수가 있지? 저렇게 입고 클럽에 오고싶나?

아예 벗고 오는게 낫겠다…

PaRam   그건 네가 바라는 거겠지!

Club Night at Hongdae

바람   Did you see that chick walk by? She's to die for!

선수   To die for? She looks like a whore. How can she dress in such a
ggoraji? She wants to come to the club dressed like that…
She might as well come naked.

바람   You wish!

꼬라지 나다

[ggo-ra-ji na-da]

get bent out of shape; be cranky, crabby or snarky

이 또한 상태를 의미하는 꼴이라는 단어와 관련이 있다. 이것은 글자 그대로'감정이 상한 상태'여기서는 성질(성깔)이 나게 된 것을 의미하는데, 성깔을 의미하는 전라도 방언'꼬라 지'로부터 유래한 표현이다.

Also coming from *ggol* (꼴), *ggorajinada* means "in bad shape" or "in poor form." Ggoraji comes from Jeolla province where it is dialect for a fierce temperament or someone who is offended over trifles and gets "bent out of shape" easily.

계산소

Areum	(점원에게) 계산해 주세요.
Minji	나 잠깐 화장실 다녀올께.
Areum	뭐라고? 언니 돌아올 때까지 계산서는 그 자리에 있을거야!!
Minji	왜 그렇게 꼬라지 났어?
Areum	아니야. 그냥 항상 내가 계산하는게 피곤해서 그래.
Minji	언니가 사줘야 더 맛있잖아. 언니이이이.

The Check

아름	(to the waiter) Check please.
민지	I'll be right back. I'm going to the rest room.
아름	What? The check will still be here when you get back!!
민지	Why are you so ggoraji nada like that?
아름	I'm not. I'm just tired of paying all the time.
민지	It's more delicious when you pay. Onni-i-i-i.

The Straight Scoop

언니이이이 [on-ni-i-i-i] or [eonni] Older sister. Koreans have a tendency to stretch out the last syllable of a word especially when they want to gain favor.

꼬붕

[ggo-bung]

a gofer or a messenger; a minion or flunky

본래, 부하를 뜻하는 일본말에서 유래한 단어이다. 이 표현은 주로 친구들 사이, 보통 남자들 사이에서 가장 센 남자의 지위를 나타내기 위해 쓰인다. 꼬붕은 졸개, 추종자와 같은 지위가 낮은 하급자를 의미한다.

Originally, a Japanese word for subordinate, *ggobung* is typically used jokingly between friends and most often among men who have established an alpha male position. A *ggobung* is an inferior, like a sidekick, a hanger-on, lackey or devotee used as a messenger or gofer by the superior and often treated like a "doormat."

배트맨과 로빈

Robin   악당이 출현했어. 꼬붕! 빨리 무찌르러 가자.

Batman   뭐? 꼬붕? 너 지금 무슨 소리 하는거야.

              이 쇼의 주인공은 나야!

Robin   이런 건방진 자식. 내가 그동안 모든 일을 해왔고 넌 그 모든 영광을 가져갔어… 이제 더이상은 안돼!!

              지금부터는 로빈과 배트맨 쇼야.

Batman   글쎄? 나는…

Robin   아무튼, 닥치고 따라와 꼬붕. 우리 할 일이 생겼어.

Batman and Robin

로빈   A ruffian has appeared. Ggobung! Let's go clobber him.

배트맨   What? Ggobung? What in tarnation are you talking about? I'm the hero of this show.

로빈   You conceited fellow. I do all the work and you take all the glory… Well no more!! From now on it's the Robin and Batman Show.

배트맨   Well? I…

로빈   Anyway, shut up and follow me, Ggobung. We've got work to do.

꼬지다

[ggo-ji-da]

to be worthless or of poor quality; a piece of shit

품질이나 성능이 다른 것에 비해 뒤떨어짐을 의미한다. 일반적으로 거지라는 단어는 부정적인 의미를 함축하고 있으므로, "거지같다!" 라는 표현에서 이와같이 변형된 것으로 추측된다.

Lower in quality and performance in comparison to other things, *ggojida* may be a bastardization of the Korean word for beggar, *geoji* (거지) due to its overall negative connotation as with describing something as *geoji*-like, scavenged or scrounged.

Synonym: 후지다 [hu-ji-da] lousy; inferior; a lemon

맥 vs. PC

PC 제기랄! 난 이 컴퓨터 진짜 싫어. 완전 꼬지다.

Mac 무슨 문제 있어? 너 산지 얼마 안됐자나?

PC 그래, 그런데 이건 일본놈들꺼야! 빌어먹을 후지쓰!

Mac 아니야, 이 인종차별쟁이야! 일본놈들꺼라서가 아니라 PC라서 그런거야. 꼬지다 꼬져.

PC 너와 너의 Mac!! 넌 그걸로 싸이월드도 못하자나.

Mac (컴퓨터를 사랑스럽게 바라보며, 노래한다) "너는 나의 눈의 사과…"

Mac vs. PC

PC Damn! I hate this computer. Totally ggojida.

맥 What's wrong? Didn't you just buy that?

PC Yeah, but it's Japanese! Fuckin' Fujitsu!

맥 No, you racist! Not because it's Japanese, because it's a PC. Ggojida, ggojyo.

PC You and your Mac!! You can't even get Cyworld to work on that.

맥 [Staring at computer lovingly, singing] "You are the Apple of my eye…"

꼴았다

[ggor-at-da]

to gamble or fritter away; to squander

돈을 가치없는 일에 낭비한다는 의미를 가지고 있는 꼬라박다라는 단어로부터 변형되어졌다. 이것은 돈을 잃는 것을 의미하는데, 보통 도박할때 돈을 왕창 잃은 경우, 돈이나 노력 따위를 한가지에 몽땅 투자해서 좋은 결과를 못 낸 경우에 사용되는 단어이다.

From *ggorabakda* (꼬라박다), which means to waste money on useless things, this was modified to *ggoratda* and means to lose money in a bet. *Ggoratda* is most often used with gambling as in to "get in too deep," but can also refer to drinking too heavily (getting plastered), or paying way too much for crap.

영계

SiWoo	와우, 저 여자 봐!
Peter	이야, 진짜 완전 귀엽다! 그런데 너보다 너무 어려.
SiWoo	아니야. 25살은 돼보여. 그리고 또 교포같애.
Peter	내기하자...
SiWoo	...젠장! 꼴았다. 이제 막 고등학교 졸업했대!
Peter	그래, 난 저런 영계 어디에서든지 알아 볼 수 있어.

Spring Chicken

시우	Wow, check her out!
피터	Yeah, she's definitely cute, but way too young for you.
시우	No way, she's got to be 25. And a kyopo as well.
피터	Let's bet...
시우	...Shit! ggoratda. She's fresh out of high school!
피터	Yeah, I can spot a spring chicken anywhere.

The Straight Scoop

교포 [kyo-po] this term refers to people of ethnic Korean ancestry who have lived the majority of their lives outside of Korea.

꼴통

[ggol-tong]

a blockhead or butthead; a retard; an ass

골통이라는 단어를 세게 발음하여 변형된 말. 골통은 글자상으로 머리를 의미하지만 속어적으로는 아무것도 모르고 한심한 짓만 해서 애를 먹이는 사람을 의미한다. 이 꼴통들은 보통 자신 뿐만 아니라 남에게도 피해를 입힌다.

Ggoltong comes from *goltong* (골통), literally meaning a head or skull and pronounced with extra emphasis on the initial 'g'. As slang, it refers to someone that does shameful things without realizing it. Such troublesome people not only harm themselves but also others.

3학년 카사노바

Kaeul	작년에 피터가 가르치지 않으셨어요?
YuJa	그 쬐그만 꼴통! 귀엽지만 정말 대책이 없는 아이죠.
Kaeul	그 꼴통같은 자식을 어떻게 해야할지 모르겠어요…
YuJa	왜요? 그 애가 또 무슨 일 저질렀나요?
Kaeul	어제 그녀석이 뛰어다니면서 모든 여자애들에게 뽀뽀를 하고 다녔어요.
YuJa	그래요, 정말 다루기 힘든 아이에요.
	오늘은 꼴통, 내일은 카사노바.

3rd Grade Casanova

가을	Didn't you have Peter in your class last year?
유자	That little ggoltong! He's a cute kid, but totally clueless.
가을	He's such a ggoltong, I don't know what to do with him…
유자	Why? What did he do this time?
가을	Yesterday he was running around kissing all the girls.
유자	Yeah, he's a handful, all right. Ggoltong today, Casanova tomorrow.

꼽사리 끼다

[ggob-sa-ri ggi-da]

to crash (a party); to butt in

이 표현을 이루는 기본 요소는 다음과 같다: 꼽 – 아마도 인색한 사람을 뜻하는 꼽꼽쟁이라는 단어로부터 유래한 것 같다. 사리 – 우연의 이익을 얻으려 하는 것을 뜻한다. 끼다 – 가담하다 또는 참가하다라는 의미이다. 이 단어들이 합쳐지면 아무도 반기지 않는 상황에 활동에 대한 돈은 고려하지 않은 채 억지로 끼어들려 하는 것을 의미한다.

The elements of this expression are as follows: *ggop* – may come from *ggop-ggop-jaeng-i* (꼽꼽쟁이) meaning an ungenerous or stingy person; *sari* - seeking profit by hook or by crook; and *ggida* – to join or take part in. All together, the meaning is to force one's way into a situation where they are otherwise unwelcome and at the same time not contribute to the payment for the activity.

보복

WonDong	오 젠장, 먼지 왔다. 그리고 오늘은 금요일이야!
DongWon	난 쟤가 또 꼽사리 낄거라고 확신해. 우리 복수하자.
WonDong	그래, 이번에는 쟤가 돈내게 하는거야.
	돈도 벌었는데 같이 낸 적 한번도 없었잖나.
DongWon	나이트에 데려간 다음에 우리는 돈 없다고 하자.
Minji	오빠! 안녕, 오늘밤에는 어디갈거야? 나이트 갈꺼지...

Payback

원동	Oh shit, here comes Meonji. And it's Friday!
동원	I bet she's going to ggobsali ggida again. Let's get her.
원동	We'll make her pay this time. She's got money but never chips in.
동원	Take her to the nightclub and tell her we have no money.
민지	Oppa! Anyeong, where are we going tonight?
	A night(club)...

48

Family Matters and Friends

The Who's Who Respective on Relatives and other Relations

♂ **오빠** [o-ppa] also [o-bba] literally an elder brother, but can be used by a female to express fondness and affection for any male, sometimes even if the male is younger.

♂ **형** [hyeong] older brother (among males; can be used for older friends)

♀ **언니** [eon-ni] older sister (among females; can be used for older friends)

♀ **누나** [nu-na] older sister (to a guy; can be used for older friends)

⚥ **동생 (남동생, 여동생)** [dong-saeng] younger sister or brother (to anyone)

⚥ **베프** [be-peu] short for best friend from 베스트 프렌드

⚥ **절친** [jeol-chin] short for closest friend from 절친한 친구

♂ **아버지** [a-beo-ji] father, also **아빠** [a-bba] dad (sorry, this cannot be used like "who's your daddy?")

♀ **어머니** [eo-meo-ni] mother, also **엄마** [eom-ma] mom

♀ **이모** [i-mo] aunt (on the mother's side)

♀ **고모** [go-mo] aunt (on the father's side), also **숙모** [sok-mo] (wife of 삼촌)

♂ **삼촌** [sam-chon] uncle (on the father's side)

♂ **외삼촌** [ui-sam-chon] uncle (on the mother's side)

The Straight Scoop

먼지 [meon-ji] meaning dust, it is a nickname for a friend named 민지 [minji] due to the similar sound.

나이트 [night-e] Koreans usually refer to a nightclub simply as "Night."

꿀벅지

[ggul-beok-ji]

honey thighs

건강하고 섹시한 여성의 다리를 지칭한다. 오랫동안 많은 사람들에게 추구되었던 삐쩍 마른 이미지 대신에 튼튼하고 근육질의 몸매를 받아들이기 시작한 신세대 용어이다.

With a hint of 'hubba hubba' and somewhat suggestively, *ggul-beok-ji* literally translates to "honey thighs" and refers to a pair of full, hearty, and super-sexy thighs in a generation that is finally embracing proud curves, with more sturdy and muscular features in place of the old-school rail-thin image that was chased by men and women for so many years.

달콤한 누나

JiTae	걔를 볼 때마다 ACDC 노래 "You Shook Me All Night Long"이 생각나.
MinShik	왜 그런데?
JiTae	가사에 있잖아, "너의 그 미국 허벅지로 나를 넘어뜨려 줘~"
MinShik	아, 걔 꿀벅지 때문에?
JiTae	그래 꿀벅지! 꿀처럼 달콤하지.
MinShik	야, 걘 네 빌어먹을 누나라고!
JiTae	꿀단지! 헤헤, 죽여주지!
MinShik	누구한테 말해야되겠어..

Sweet Sister

지태   Every time, I see her, I think of that ACDC song: "You Shook Me All Night Long"

민식   Why is that?

지태   It's right there in the lines: "knockin' me out with those American thighs."

민식   Oh, because of her ggul-beok-ji?

지태   Yeah, ggul-beok-ji! Sweet as honey!

민식   She's your fucking sister, man!

지태   Jugs of honey! He he! Totally to die for!

민식   I gotta tell someone about this...

The Straight Scoop

죽인다 [jug-in-da] literally meaning to kill or murder, here this expression is used to describe something or someone as extremely good or desirable, often with the implication of sexy or hot. Very similar to the English expression "to die for."

꼽살리다

[ggob-sal-li-da]

to bug, bother, irritate or annoy; get under one's skin

문자 그대로는 '겁이나게 하다, 겁이나게 만들다.'는 의미로서 이는 주로 특정 인물을 심하게 놀리는 행위를 일컫는 말이다. 보통 친한 친구들사이에서 사용된다.

Literally, to revive someone or make them live, *sal-li-da* (살리다) is combined with *ggob* (꼽) suggesting that the subject is brought back to life through fear. This is most often used between close friends to tease each other or "get under their skin."

엘비스는 살아있다

WonDong	미구! 이 미친 구렛나루야. 구렛나루 좀 짤러라.
TaeYong	그만 좀 꼽살려. 불쌍해. 미구 표정좀 봐.
	조금 더 하면 울 것 같애.
DongWon	됐어. 이제 저자식이 꼽살리는거 적응됐어.

Elvis Lives

원동	Migu! Look at your crazy sideburns.
	Trim those things up.
태용	Quit ggopsal~ing him. Look at Migu's expression.
	Do it any more and he'll cry!
동원	That's enough. I'm used to that SOB's ggopsal.

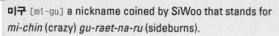

The Straight Scoop

미구 [mi-gu] a nickname coined by SiWoo that stands for *mi-chin* (crazy) *gu-raet-na-ru* (sideburns).

The Annoyingly
Nasal Nìun

From right to left,
it angles tongue up, the tip thrust high
for words bereft of voice,
letting the nasal n linger, oh my
Incessantly on in a never-ending whinny
ㄴㄴㄴㄴㄴ (ne ne ne ne ne)
The undeniably annoying nìun ⌣ ninny

나발불다
[na-bal-bul-da]

swig it; suck it down; brown bag it; knock back

축어적으로, 나팔을 연주하는 것을 의미. 과거에는 일반적으로 사용되지 않았던 방식으로 이것은 술을 병째로 마시는 것을 표현하는 것이다. (나팔을 부는 모습과 흡사하다고 하여 이렇게 일컫게 됨)

Literally, to play the trumpet, this refers to the habit of drinking alcohol straight from a bottle (putting your lips to the trumpet, so to speak), which was not commonly acceptable until recent times in Korea because manners dictated that one should pour into and drink from a glass. This expression is similar in connotation to the English practice of "brown bagging it" though closer in meaning to "knock one back" or "knock back a cold one."

1차, 2차, 3차 기절

SiWoo	벌써 많이 취했네? 많이 마셨어?
MinHee	응, 이게 3차째야.
HeeYeon	시우 왔옹? 나 안보고 싶었옹? 왜 이제와아아아앙~
SiWoo	도도한 회연이가 왜이래? 회연이 술 안 좋아하잖아.
MinHee	무슨 도도한 회연... 얘 1차부터 나발불고, 2차 때는 코르넷 불었다가 지금은 잭다니엘을 병째로 불고있는 것 봐!

1-cha, 2-cha, 3-cha, Drop

시우	You're already totally drunk? Did you drink a lot?
민희	Eung, this is 3-cha.
회연	SiWoo-ya you came? Didn't you miss me-e-e-e? Why you come now-w-w?
시우	Why is our proud HeeYeon like this? She doesn't even like drinking?
민희	What proud HeeYeon? From 1-cha she was nabalbulda, by 2cha she played the Cornet and now look at her trumpeting with that bottle of Jack!

Culturally Speaking

1-cha, 2-cha, 3-cha, drop!
The Stages of Korean drinking

Koreans rarely drink at home, except with family and so when drinking with friends or coworkers, they must go out. Socializing with Korean businessmen after hours usually means a series of drinking rounds and changing venues. The first round, or 1-cha in Korean, usually involves a meal and some soju. 2-cha, or second stage, often entails a change to whiskey and beer. And in 3-cha almost anything goes — and it's likely that you won't remember anyway.

Luckily, there is often a chance to bow out between stages and especially between the 2nd and 3rd stages. Otherwise you might have trouble waking up the next morning to attend an important business meeting or catch a flight.

Note: Most Koreans think that it is impolite to drink alcohol straight from a bottle. Soju bottles, which are about the size of a 12 oz. beer bottle, are poured into small shot glasses with many specific mannerisms. And until recently, most beer bottles in Korea were much larger in size and rather awkward to drink out of.

The Straight Scoop

옹, 옹 & 아아아앙 [ong, ong & a-a-a-ang] Korean girls often use such endings to be cute or put on a display of winsome innocence.

나비

[na-bi]

a flirt or cocktease; to toy with someone

본래 나비를 의미, 나비는 꽃가루를 수집하기 위해서 꽃에서 꽃으로 옮겨다닌다. 이런 점에서, 이 여자(여기서 나비는 여자만 의미)는 잠재적인 다른 남성들로부터 관심이나 칭찬을 받기 위해 그들에게 어떠한 만족도 주지 않으며 장난삼아 연애를 하는 사람이다.

Originally a butterfly, a *nabi* goes from flower to flower collecting pollen. In this sense, she (for a butterfly can only refer to a girl) is a flirt collecting compliments or attention from potential suitors while not giving them any satisfaction. The male equivalent would be to *ggot-bat-ae non-da* (꽃밭에 논다) or to play in a flower field.

지붕관찰 (홍대 편)

Bill 이거 본 적 있어? 저 아래, 이쪽 저쪽 얼쩡거리며 다니고 있는 금요일 저녁 나비들 보이지?

Ted 그래, 외롭고 절망적인 사랑받지 못하는 사람들에게는 또 다른 슬픈 밤이지.

Bill 그럼 저 쪽에 내려가서 쟤들 놀려주자! 우리가 꽃가루 없는 꽃들이 되는거야.

Ted 훌륭해! 나비 응징.

Rooftop Review (Hongdae Edition)

빌 Have you seen this? Down there, you can see the Friday night nabis flirting as they make their way down the block.

테드 Yeah, another sad night for the desperate and loveless.

빌 Let's get down there and tease them then! We'll be flowers with no pollen.

테드 Excellent!... Nabi retribution.

나이롱 환자 ☕

[na-i-rong hwan-ja]

nylon patient; scam artist

천연의 물질이 아닌 나이롱, 이와 같이 나이롱 환자는 "자연적으로" 또는 실제로 아픈 것이 아닌 무언가 이익을 기대하고 아픈 척 하는 사람이다. 이 표현은 교통사고를 당하고 보상을 기대하여 다친 척 하는 사람을 일컬을때 종종 사용된다.

Nylon is not a natural substance. As such, a *nairong hwanja* or nylon patient relates to someone who is not "naturally" or truthfully hurt, but fakes an injury or feigns sickness or for some monetary or other benefit. It is often used for someone who is in a car accident and pretends to be injured to get compensation.

Also: 나이롱 신자 [na-i-rong shin-ja] a false believer or sham churchgoer (someone who attends church merely for the social network, but is not a real believer).

흰 나이롱

SiWoo	사고 당했다고 들었어. 많이 다쳤어?
Peter	아니, 별로.
SiWoo	그럼, 나이롱 환자 된거야?
Peter	아니, 그런 짓 절대 안해! 이걸로 돈 버는거 아니야!
SiWoo	그럼 여기서 뭐해?
Peter	글쎄, 난 섹시한 간호사들의 흰 나이롱 스타킹에 약하잖아?

White Nylons

시우	I heard you were in an accident. You hurt bad?
피터	No, not really.
시우	Well, then are you being a nylon hwanja?
피터	No, I would never do that! I'm not getting money for this!
시우	Then what are you doing here?
피터	Well, I'm a sucker for all these hot nurses in their white nylons!

나와바리

[na-wa-ba-ri]

one's hood or turf; a managing district

1950년대 즈음 깡패들은 그들의 영향력이 미치는 그들만의 특정한 구역이 있었는데 이러한 구역이나 지역을 의미하는 일본어로부터 유래한 말이다. 다른 사람들이 방문하면 그 지역에 거주하고 있는 사람이 대접하길 원하는 상황과 같은 경우 이 속어를 사용한다. "이곳은 내 나와바리니까 내가 쏠게."

From the Japanese for a zone or (managing) district, *nawabari* refers to one's area, hood, turf or stomping grounds, particularly in the 1950's sense of a gang's area of influence. In such a situation, the host who says this may be indicating that since the other person is visiting his neighborhood, the host wishes to foot the bill: "It's my *nawabari*, so I'll pay."

웰컴투 창현 골

ChangHyun	나의 나와바리에 온 것을 환영해... 오늘밤 내가 한턱 쏜다.
SiWoo	이야~ 창현이한테 이런 면이 있는 줄 몰랐네.
Peter	나도. 우리가 창현이를 잘못 생각했던것 같애.
ChangHyun	난, 멋진 김두환이다.

〔2시간 후 (모두 배불리 먹고 마신 뒤)〕

ChangHyun	나 이제 가봐야겠다, 너희들끼리 재밌게 놀다 가.
SiWoo	(창현이가 계산대로 갔을 때) 이야 오늘 대박이다!
Peter	(막잔) 화끈한 창현이를 위해. 이제 가자.
Waiter	잠시만요, 계산 안 하셨는데요!
Peter	계산 안 하고갔네, 깎아달라고만 말했대! 결국 깎지도 못했어!
Siwoo	나의 나와바리, 구라였어.

Welcome to Changhyun Gol

창현   Welcome to my nawabari… Tonight, I'll shoot.

시우   Wow, I didn't know ChangHyun had it in him.

피터   Me neither. I guess we misjudged him.

창현   Me, I'm a regular Kim DuHwan.

[2 hours later (all are drunk and full)]

창현   I've got to go, but relax and enjoy yourselves.

시우   (as ChangHyun goes to the counter) We hit the jackpot tonight!

피터   (Last glass) Here's to ChangHyun, a great host. Let's go.

점원   Wait, you haven't paid!

피터   He didn't pay, he only asked for a discount!
            And didn't even get one!

시우   My nawabari, my ass.

The Straight Scoop

한턱 쏜다 [han-teok sson-da] I'll shoot, similar to "It's my treat." Meaning I'll pay.

김두환 [Kim DuHwan] a famous mob boss from the 1950's who later became a politician.

대박 [dae-bak] to hit the jackpot. See page 80.

낙동강 오리알

[nak-dong-gang ori al]

a pathetic person; a sad story; an abandoned duck egg

낙동강, 부산 외곽을 감싸고 있는 강으로 한국 전쟁 시작 직후 마지막 방어선이었던 곳. 한 반도의 가장 밑부분, 아무것도 없는 작고 외로운 막다른 지역이 수비를 위한 지역이 되었다. 불쌍한 낙동강 오리알 같은. 그래서 매우 불쌍한 외로운 사람을 낙동강 오리알이라고 부른다(보통 친구들 사이에서 장난 칠때 쓰인다). 비슷한 영어식 표현으로는 "Here I sit like a bird in the wilderness" 가 있다.

The Nakdong River, on the outskirts of Busan, was the last line of defense for the South Korean and US forces shortly after the beginning of the Korean War. Driven to the very bottom of the peninsula, there was nothing but a small, lonely section left to defend; a 'poor, duck egg' of sorts. So a poor, lonely person is called a *nakdong-gang orial* or a Nakdong River duck egg (usually used teasingly between friends); a lonesome bird of sorts. Somewhat similar to the English expression: "Here I sit like a bird in the wilderness."

강 알 시

서울을 유랑하다
낙동강 오리알을 보았네.
돌담에 기대어 자리잡고있는
구멍 안에 감춰져 있는

어둠의 그의 슬픔을 통하여
여자는 그 남자를 미치게 만들고

친구, 나는 너를 그렇게 부른다
무슨 문제가 있어 넌 알이 된거니
기쁨에 가득찬 뜨거운
연회를 즐겼지만 넌 그녀를 만나지 못한거니?

그녀는 나에게 전화를 하겠다고 약속했지만
전화는 오지 않았고 나는 지금 낙동강 오리알

Ode to a River Egg

In my stroll through Seoul
I saw a nakdonggang ori-al
Perched against a wall
Of stone, almost hidden in a hole

Of darkness, sifting through his sadness
A woman near driven him to madness

Friend, I called out, what troubles you so
To make an egg of you, though
Yesterday, we reveled in the heat
Of your joy that you did her meet?

"She made me a promise to call
But didn't and now I am a nakdonggang ori-al."

낙하산

[nak-ha-san]

parachute nepotism; preferential treatment; pull strings

통속적으로 파라슈트라는 의미를 가지고 있는 낙하산은 자식에게 유리한 지위 또는 특혜의 영향을 주는 부모 또는 정책적인 연계를 일컫기 위해 비속어로 사용되었다. 이 표현은 직장인들이 연고주의를 나타내기 위해 사용하였고 보통 부정적인 질투 혹은 적개심을 나타낸다.

Literally meaning a parachute, *nakhasan* became slang for the influence of ones parents or political connections being used to gain a favorable position or preferential treatment. This expression is used by employees to describe such nepotism in a negative light due to envy or resentment. It vaguely alludes to the English "golden parachute," "pull strings for someone," or even just some "lucky bastard" who was born with a "silver spoon" in his mouth.

낙하산 사이즈

SoYoon   신입 쟤 뭐야? 어떻게 쟤가 우리보다 윗자리로 간거야?

                       누군가를 알고 있는게 분명해.

ChangHyun   쟤 낙하산이라고 들었어. 저 남자 아버지가 신이야.

SoYoon   롯데? 난 낙하산 진짜 싫어.

ChangHyun   뭐? 너도 너희 아버지가 이 직장 얻어주신거 아니야?

                       아버지가 이사님이시잖아... 너는 그냥 화난거겠지.

                       그가 너보다 큰 낙하산이라서.

SoYoon   닥치지 않으면 넌 곧 하늘에서 떨어지게 될거야!

The Straight Scoop

신 [shin] Shin, here can have dual meaning. First, it means a god or demigod, but it also happens to be the family name of the CEO of the Lotte Group (a large conglomerate in Korea).

Parachute Size

소윤   Who is this new guy? How did he get positioned above us?
        He must know someone.

창현   Yeah, I heard he is a nakhasan. His father is a Shin.

소윤   From Lotte? God I hate nakhasan.

창현   What? Didn't your dad get you this job?
        He's a senior manager... You're just mad because
        he has a bigger parachute.

소윤   Shut up or you're going to fall from the sky!

Culturally Speaking

The Old Boy's Network

Nepotism in Korea is not a problem... it is a way of life. Much of Korean society and business culture is based on relationships: family relations; relationships from school; and regional ties. For instance, if you want a job at the Jungang Daily Newspaper, you'd better be a graduate of Seoul National University. Such favoritism or partisanship would merely be seen as "looking after one's own."

낚다

[nakk-da]

to hook someone; "you got me"

문자 그대로 물고기를 낚는 것을 의미하는 이 표현은 다른 사람을 속이거나 속임 당하는
것을 뜻하는 속어이다. "아 또 낚였다"와 같이 주로 수동태로 쓰인다. 또한 농담을 하고
"낚였지?" 라고 말할 수도 있다. 이성을 침대로 꼬시거나 부유한 사람을 낚는다는 의미로
쓰일 수도 있다.

Literally "to catch a fish," *nakkda* is used as slang for fooling or tricking someone.
Usually used in the passive form, as in "Ah, I got duped again" or "You got me." but
can be used by the person doing the gag, "I had you going didn't I?" (*nakk-yeot-ji?*).
Nakkda is also sometimes used for luring a partner into bed, most often for 'hooking'
a (wealthy) man or woman.

만우절 생선

Psy   생선피, 생선 피… 시장의 세 물고기에 대해 들어본 적 있어?

GeunHye   무슨 말 하는 거야? 낚시라도 가니?

Psy   낚으러 가는 거 맞아! 시장의 물고기 세마리. 빨간 생선, 파란 생선,
그리고 노란 생선의 머리가 잘려 나갔어. 걔네 피가 무슨 색깔이게?
맞히면 내가 너에 대한 노래 만들어 줄게.

GeunHye   글쎄, 빨간 생선은 빨간색이겠지, 맞지?

Psy   딩동! 그리고 파란 생선 피는?

GeunHye   파란색…?

Psy   와, 너 이거 정말 잘한다! 좋아, 이제 노래까지 한번 더!

GeunHye   그리고 노란 생선은 바닥에 노란 피를 뿌리겠지!

Psy   땡! 미안. 노란 생선은 붕어빵이었어. 푸하하하!

GeunHye   아, 싸이씨… 또 낚였네! 넌 날 맨날 낚아!

April Fools Fish

싸이   Fish blood, fish blood... have you heard the one about the three fish in the market?

근혜   What are you talking about? You going fishing?

싸이   Nakkda's right! Three fish in the market: a red one, a blue one and a yellow one get their heads chopped off [ouch]. What color is their blood? Guess right, and I'll make a song about you.

근혜   Well, the red one is obviously red, right?

싸이   Ding-dong! And the blue one's blood?

근혜   Blue...?

싸이   Wow, you're so good at this! Great job!
    ...Now one more for the song.

근혜   And the yellow one spurts --- yellow blood on the floor!

싸이   Ddeng! Sorry. The yellow fish blood is black!
    It's bungobbang! Buhahaha!

근혜   Ah, Psy-shi... Again, nakkyotnae! You fool me every time!

The Straight Scoop

딩동 or 딩동댕 [ding-dong-dang] the sound of winning... You got it right!

땡 [ddeng] the sound of losing, like the "eeeh" of a game show buzzer. (Oddly, in another context this word can indicate a lucky break.)

붕어빵 [bung-o-bbanng] a common treat (usually for children) made with yellow waffle bread that has red bean paste inside and is formed to look like a fish.

네똥 굵다

[nui-ddong geulk-da]

your poop is thick; your shit don't stink

문자 그대로의 의미는 너의 배설물이 두껍고 크다라는 의미, 이 표현은 자기 자랑이 심한 사람이나 자기 착각에 빠져 사는 사람들에게 주로 사용된다. 영어로 비슷한 표현으로는 "네 똥은 냄새 안나냐?" 라는 표현이 있다.

Literally meaning "your poop is thick," *nui-ddong geulk-da* is used in a patronizing way to a bragger, snob or someone who is otherwise full of himself or herself. In English, a similar expression would be "You think your shit doesn't stink?"

굵기가 중요해?

Victor	...그리고 특별장학금도 받고 하버드 대학교 입학 허가 사무실에서 오래.
DongWon	그래, 그래, 네똥 굵다. 그렇게 똥이 굵어서 변기는 안막히냐?
Victor	우리집에서 똥이 굵고 안 굵고는 중요하지 않아. 우리집 변기는 절대 막히지 않거든.
DongWon	뭐? 그게 무슨 말이야? 이번에는 집 좋다고 자랑하는거야?
Victor	사실은 나 시골에서 살거든. 우리집 변기 푸세식이야.

Does Thickness Count?

빅터	...and then I was awarded a fellowship, after being scouted out by the admissions office at Harvard.
동원	All right, all right, nuiddong geulkda. As such, your toilets must be clogged with your thick poop.
빅터	At my house it doesn't matter if my poop is thick or not. The toilets at my house can't be clogged.
동원	What? What are you saying? Now you are bragging that your house is better?
빅터	Actually, I live in the countryside... I use an outhouse.

The Poop Box

 Koreans are fascinated by poop...they talk about it, draw it, and children love to try to poke you in the anus, gleefully shouting "*ddong chim*" (poop acupuncture).

Poop 응가 [eung-ga] a baby's onomatopoeic expression for poop.

Poop belly 똥배 [ddong-bae] a pot belly (connotation is cute)

Poop acupuncture 똥침 [ddong-chim] children in Korea have a particular affinity for putting their hands together, folding their fingers in the form of a gun, and sneaking up behind a person to (playfully?) jab them in the anus.

Poop dog 똥개 [ddong-gae] a street dog (dogs will often eat their own poop)

Poop dog training 똥개훈련 [ddong-gae-hun-ryeol]sending someone on errands, as if a dog fetching something (often used in military service).

Poop pigs 똥돼지 [ddong-duae-ji] pigs fed with human excrement (particularly those from Jeju island), thought to be particularly delicious in Korea – eew!

Poop puppy 똥강아지 [ddong-gang-a-ji] my little mutt (usually from a grandparent - people would call thier children by unflattering names to keep jealous ghosts or spirits away, Boo!)

The price of poop 똥값 [ddong-gap] something particularly cheap

Poop water 똥물 [ddong-mul] dirty water (mostly for a river, lake or the sea). The Han river was particularly poop-ridden but has been cleaned up in recent years.

Stubborn poop 똥고집 [ddong-go-jib] stubbornness without reason.

Your poop is thick 네똥 굵다 [nui-ddong geulk-da] described above.

Poop dream 똥꿈 [ddong geum] dream of poop and you will have good luck (also true for dreaming of a pig. Hmmm...).

So poor, his poop hole is torn 똥구녕이 찢어지게 가난하다 [ddong-gu-nyeong-i jjij-eo-ji-gae ga-nan-ha-da] self explanatory (as poor as shit).

날라리

[nal-la-ri]

a player or a punk; a hoodlum; a juvenile delinquent

본래 솜(오보에의 전신인 목관악기)을 의미하지만 젊은 사람들은 공부하지 않고 장난치는 것에만, 혹은 여자나 또는 남자나 외모에만 관심있는 사람을 일컬을 때 사용한다.

Originally "a shawm" (the predecessor to the oboe), but to young people, a *nallari* is a person who doesn't often study and cares only for having fun, clubbing, drinking, smoking, and of course, the opposite sex.

김치를 담그며

Ajumma1	유진이는 아직도 그... 그 남자애 만나?
Ajumma2	어...
Ajumma1	걔 날라리같던데... 왜 그 애 만나지 못하게 막지 않아?
Ajumma2	나도 알아, 하지만 그 녀석 정말 잘 생겼거든. 김치 담글 때 마늘 못 빼듯이 그 날라리 만나는 걸 막는 것은 어려워.
Ajumma1	그래, 나는 그 녀석이 유진이의 인생에 양념이 될 거라고 생각해... 유진이가 우리같이 늙고 김치 만들때 기억할 추억거리가 될거야.

Making Kimchi

아줌마1	Is YuJin still seeing that... that boy?
아줌마2	Yes...
아줌마1	He's such a nalari... why don't you forbid her to see him?
아줌마2	I know, but he's so handsome. You might as well take the garlic out of kimchi as protect her from that nalari.
아줌마1	Yeah, I guess he will add flavor to her life... Something for her to remember when she is old and making kimchi like us.

넨장맞을

[naen-jang-maj-eul]

it's torture; cursed; damn; oh the agony!

문자 그대로의 의미는 난장을 맞아야 할 놈 이라는 뜻이다. 난장은 조선왕조 (1392-1910), 사람을 발가벗긴채 곤장을 치는 고문의 일종이다. 이 속어는 좋지 않은 상황에서는 언제든지 사용될 수 있으며, 또한 사람에게 직접적으로도 쓰일 수 있다. "이런 넨장맞을 놈." 속어, "젠장"과 비슷한 의미로 쓰인다.

Literally "you should be beaten like *nanjang* (난장)." *Nanjang* is a style of torture from the time of the Joseon dynasty (1392-1910), where a naked person is beaten. It can be used for any unpleasant situation or even directed at a person as: "You should be tortured." It would be similar to "Oh, shit" or the old expression: "Tie me to an anthill and cover me with jam."

화장실 이야기

DongWon	야 뚱땡이… 왜 우리랑 같이 먹으러 안가?
Victor	나 문제가 있어. 아, 넨장맞을!
DongWon	소화불량?
Victor	아니, 나 먹는게 두려워… 나 곧 집에 가봐야하는데, 우리 푸세식 변기가 꽉 찼거든.

Toilet Talk

동원	Hey fatty… Why aren't you eating with us?
빅터	I have a problem. Ah, naenjangmajeul!
동원	Indigestion?
빅터	No, I'm afraid to eat… I have to go home soon, and my outhouse is full.

노가다

[no-ga-da]

to do hard work; needlessly toil

본래는 공사판에서 하는 막일을 의미한다. 하지만, 속어적으로 이것은 모든 힘든일을 일컬을 때 비유적으로 사용된다.

Originally meaning "construction work," but expanded in the lexicon of young people to mean any kind of hard work or arduous endeavor ahead of them. *Nogada* is most often used for what one might consider menial work or a pointless effort.

Synonym: 개고생 [gae-go-saeng] an unnecessarily difficult task (lit. a dog's endeavor)

류 교수

Siwoo 류 교수 수업 넣었어? 으, 안돼!

ChangHyun 뭐? 왜?

Siwoo 완전히 노가다야. 좆나 노가다!

ChangHyun 진짜? 젠장.

Siwoo 그래, 여자친구, 술 마시는 것, 모든 것을 잊어야 해.

A학점 받길 원한다면, 아니, 단지 네가 패스하길 원한다고 해도

그의 수업에서 살고 숨 쉬어야 해. 불쌍한 창현!

노가다는 네 운명.

Professor Lew

시우 You have professor Lew? Oh, no!

창현 What? Why?

시우 Absolutely nogada. Fucking nogada!

창현 Really? That sucks.

시우 Yeah, forget girlfriends, forget drinking, forget everything.

You want an A, hell, you just want to pass, you'll have to live and

breathe his class. Poor ChangHyun! Nogada is your destiny.

노가리 까다

[no-ga-ri gga-da]

chew the fat; shoot the shit

노가리는 본래 명태 새끼를 의미한다. 한국인들은 보통 술을 마실 때 말린 노가리를 안주 삼아 먹는다. 그러므로 노가리 까다는 문자그대로 "말린 노가리를 뜯다"가 된다. 술을 마실 때 수다를 많이 떠는 것 처럼 killing time 또는 shooting the shit 을 암시한다.

A *nogari* is originally "a young walleye," which in dried form is often eaten as a side dish when drinking alcohol. Thereby, *nogari ggada* would literally be "to pare dried fish." The implication is that people tell stories while drinking, or when they have nothing else to do... like "killing time," "chewing the fat" or just "shooting the shit."

Synonym: 뒹굴뒹굴 [duing-gol-duing-gol] kill time (aimlessly surf the internet)

이상한 물고기

MyongTae	동태는 어딨어?
SaengTae	그 특이한 놈은 언제나 늦는 거 너도 알잖아.
	항상 우리를 기다리게 만들고.
MyongTae	할 것도 없는데 여기 앉아서 노가리나 까자.
SaengTae	그래, 그냥 여기 앉아서 걔 올때까지 그 자식 뒤땅이나 까고 있자.

Strange Fish

명태	Where is DongTae?
생태	You know that fish, he's always late.
	He likes to keep us on ice all the time.
명태	There's nothing to do but sit here and nogari ggada.
생태	Yeah, we'll just sit here and talk shit about that SOB till he gets here.

눈깔이 삐었다

[noon-ggal-i bbi-ot-da]

are your eyes sprained?; ya fuckin' blind?!

보통 동물들의 눈을 일컫는 단어 '눈깔'과 발목이 접지르다와 같은 경우에 쓰이는 단어 '삐다'가 결합된 말. 평범하지 않은 괴상한 취향이나 안목을 가진 사람에게 주로 사용한다.

Here, the word for eyes (*noonggal*) is one usually used for animals, indicating a lower form of language, and is combined with the word for sprain, wrench, or twist (*bbiotda*). This gives the impression of one who is without discernment or can't distinguish between pretty and ugly (read - beer goggles) with regard to a girl or boy, a car, a friend, etc.

초록 눈의 동양인

SoYoon	그만 쳐다봐... 너무 무서워!
JiYoon	왜? 내가 너무 예뻐?
SoYoon	넌 그럼 싸이보그가 예뻐? 그놈의 컬러렌즈 좀 빼라.
JiYoon	나 이거 방금 산건데... 나 신비롭게 보이지 않아?
SoYoon	넌 눈만 나쁜게 아니라 눈깔까지 삐었구나.
JiYoon	나 라식도 해야할지 몰라... 그리고 쌍꺼풀도.
SoYoon	니나니노!

The Straight Scoop

쌍커풀 [ssang-ka-pul] literally meaning eyelids, this is used to describe a plastic surgical procedure to reproduce the fold in eyelids common to Westerners.

니나니노 [ni-na-ni-no] has no literal meaning. Rather, if the letters are combined, ni (니) combined with na (나) and ni (니) combined with no (노) in a top and bottom configuration, it reveals the word babo (fool) (바보). 글자 그대로는, 아무 의미도 없다. 단지, 글자 니와 나 그리고 글자 니와 노를 위 아래로 배치하면 단어 바보를 나타내게 된다.

바 보

Green Eyed Asian

소윤   Stop looking at me... You're scaring me!

지윤   Why? I look too pretty?

소윤   If you think a cyborg is pretty! Take those things off.

지윤   I just bought these lenses. Don't they make me look mysterious?

소윤   Not only are your eyes bad, but your noonggali bbiotda too.

지윤   Maybe I should get LASIK... and ssankapul.

소윤   Nina nino!

Culturally Speaking

What the Fuck... Let's Nip and Tuck!

Plastic surgery, literally "form shaping surgery," is common and widely accepted in Korea, especially the eyes, nose, and cheekbones (more facial restructuring than the nip and tuck typical in the West). Due to flatter noses than caucasians, Koreans often choose to enlarge theirs. As such, "that's some honker," which would be an insult in the West, is a compliment in Korea.

눈탱이가 밤탱이 되다
[noon-taeng-i-ga bam-taeng-i dwe-da]

get a black eye; have a shiner

문자 그대로의 의미는 눈이 밤처럼 되다라는 뜻이다. 밤과 같이 진한 갈색(또는 구워졌을 때의 검정색)을 띄고 있으며, 의미는 눈에 멍이 들다라는 뜻이다. 한국인들은 리듬감 있는 이 표현을 좋아한다.

Literally "your eyeballs have become chestnuts." As chestnuts are dark brown (or black when roasted), the meaning of *noon-taeng-i-ga bam-taeng-i dwe-da* is to get a black eye. Koreans like this expression for its rhythm.

남자는 남자답게 산다 2

KwangSung 그 체대애랑의 싸움은 어떻게 되는거지?

우리가 무엇 때문에 그렇게 눈탱이가 밤탱이 된거야?

HwaSeok 그건 모두 밤색 머리 여자때문이야.

KwangSung 이게 모두 그 영계때문이라고? 음, 그렇게 가치있는 애구나.

HwaSeok 야 늑대, 그 여자애한테 가까이 가면 다른 눈탱이도 밤탱이가 될거야.

Boys will be Boys 2

광성 So what was this fight with the Phys Ed student over anyway? What was so important that we both got noontaengiga bamtaengi?

화석 It's all over a girl with chestnut hair.

광성 All this over a chick!? Well, she had better be worth it.

화석 Hey wolf, you go near her and your other noontaengiga bamtaengi dwelkoya.

The Over Box

A Maniac, Monger, Freak or Fiend

The Endings – ~쟁이, ~탱이, ~생이, ~돌이, ~꾸러기
Stemming from a jang-i (쟁이) or a specialist, these suffixes are used to describe a particular trait or habit, often to suggest that they do something way too much, and used in a somewhat disparaging way, to mock or belittle as a fanatic or an addict.

- **고집쟁이** [go-jib-jaeng-i] a stubborn, obstinate, hardheaded individual.

- **담탱이** [dam-taeng-i] a homeroom teacher, similar to calling someone "teach."

- **멋쟁이** [meot-jaeng-i] a person who always looks cool, a classy dresser.

- **못땡이** [mot-ddaeng-i] someone who consistently does poorly (or doesn't do what he/she should at any given time.

- **심술쟁이** [shim-sul-jaeng-i] an ill-natured person, a crank, constantly cross

- **욕심쟁이** [yok-shim-jaeng-i] a greedy, rapacious, or materialistic person, a greed head

- **잠탱이** [jam-taeng-i] a heavy-eyed person asleep on their feet, a sleepyhead.

- **점쟁이** [jeom-jaeng-i] a palm-reading, crystal gazer; a fortune-telling psychic, seer or southsayer.

- **짠돌이** [jjan-dol-i] a miser, a skinflint, a penny-pinching tightwad.

- **쫌생이** [jjom-saeng-i] a narrow-minded person, from jom, [좀] a person that slowly destroys from within, like a bookworm or clothes moth. As with someone who buys a coffee for a friend and then says: "Who am I, I'm the one who bought coffee yesterday."
  Similar expressions: **쫀쫀하다** [jjon-jjon-ha-da], **쪼잔하다** [jjo-jan-ha-da]

The Straight Scoop

늑대 [neuk-dae] literally a wolf and similar to the English "a shark," for a man always trying to pick up women. Happy hunting, fellas. Woop, woop, wooooo!

농땡이
[nong-ddaeng-i]

a slacker; a goof-off; an idler or lazybones

재미, 장난을 뜻하는 농이라는 단어가 땡이라는 접미사와 결합되어 만들어진 말. 축어적으로, 다른 사람들은 열심히 일 할 동안에 노는 사람을 의미하는 등 부정적인 의미를 함축하고 있고 이것은 종종 동사 치다와 함께 쓰여진다.

Nong (농), meaning sport, fun or play, is combined with the ending *~ddaengi* (땡이). Literally "a person that plays while others are working hard," it has a negative connotation and is often used as a verb with *chida* (치다) to play or hit. Similar to the English expressions: "goof off" or "fuck around."

대장 농땡이

HwaSeok	대장 농땡이 어디갔어?
ByungShik	창현? 열심히 일하고있어. 하! 아마 평소대로 자고 있을거야!
HwaSeok	할 일 있을 때는 절대 나타나지 않아.
ByungShik	그 귀차니스트 농땡이. 걔는 아무것도 안해!
HwaSeok	어, 충성! 언제 오셨습니까?
ChangHyun	니들 뒤땅듣고 충분히 피곤해질만큼은 됐어. 별로 커피나 뽑아와.
ByungShik	와우, 벌 주는것도 귀찮아서 커피 사오라는것은 진짜 농땡이다.

Corporal Nongddaengi

화석	Where's corporal Nongddaengi?
병식	ChangHyun? Working hard. Ha! Probably sleeping as usual!
화석	Never around when there's work to do.
병식	That guichanist nongddaengi. He never does anything!
화석	Uh, Sir! How long have you been here?
창현	Long enough to be tired of your shit. Go get me a coffee.
병식	Wow, he's too much of a nongddaengi to even punish us!

Digut's Depth Revealed

Don't deign to decide about digut ㄷ
until the letter's depth is revealed.
Tongue tipped on mouth-top put,
    unaspirated, yet plosive it peeled.
From two swift strokes, digut shoots out soft.
        Deftly drawn for 다디 (daddy),
        Yet doubly difficult in its double d,
and kinda ㄸ ㄸ ㄸ dangerous too.

대가리

[dae-ga-ri]

a bully or bruiser; a scrapper; the best brawler

글자 그대로, 머리를 의미. 머리는 신체의 가장 중요한 부분으로서 대가리는 그룹의 우두 머리를 뜻하게 되었고 특별히 초등학교나 중학교의 짱을 일컫는 말이 되었다. 그러므로, 이 표현은 초등학생 또는 중학생이 주로 사용한다.

Literally "a (big) head." As a head (used informally) is the most important part of a body, *daegari* came to describe a captain of a group, but more particularly, the best fighter in a group. This expression is used primarily by elementary or middle school students and may often be used to describe a bully, but could also be simply an accomplished brawler or someone who uses their presence to make others believe them to be.

학교원정

Victor   누가 이 학교 대가리야? 빨리 튀어나와!

KyoWul   내가 대가리인데…

Victor   뭐? 네가? 전혀 강해보이지 않는데. 아무튼 좋다. 한판 붙자!

[잠시 후]

Victor   임마! 너 싸움 전혀 못하네! 많이 아파?

KyoWul   엉엉! 왜 때려? 대가리는 내 머리가 크다고 애들이 지어준 별명이란 말이야.

An Away Match

빅터   Who is the daegari of this school? Get out here!

겨울   I'm a daegari…

빅터   What? You? You don't look so tough.
Whatever, OK. Let's go!

[a few minutes later]

빅터   Hey man! You can't fight at all! Are you hurt?

겨울   Ung ung! (crying) Why did you hit me?
Daegari is my nickname, because I have a huge head.

대략난감
[dae-ryak-nan-gam]

a pain in the ass; a total drag; unbearable

문자 그대로의 의미는 대략적으로 참을 수 없다, 혹은 견딜 수 없다라는 뜻. 이 표현은 듣는 사람을 재미없게 만드는 긴 이야기 후, 주로 채팅상에서 종종 사용된다. "너의 이야기를 듣는 것은 정말 난감하다" 라는 의미로 썰렁하다라는 표현과 비슷하게 사용된다.

Literally meaning "roughly speaking" (*dae-ryak*) and "to be intolerable or unbearable" (*nan-gam*). The phrase is used, following a long story that the listener seems to find uninteresting especially when chatting online, to say "listening to your story was unbearable" or "a real snooze." It is similar to *sollonghada* (썰렁하다), which means "it's boring." It can also be used to express something like "aint that a bitch!"

농담 따먹기

WonDong   …그리고나서 승려가 성직자에게 말했어. "떡볶이 좋아해?" 하 하 하 하… 알았지? 그녀는 땡추야.

DongWon   아이고! 대략난감!

Just in Jest or Down in the Doldrums

원동   …And then the Buddhist nun said to the monk, "Do you like ddokbboki?" Ha ha ha ha… Get it? She was a ddaengchu!

동원   Oh my! Daeryak-nangam!

The Straight Scoop

떡볶이 [ddok-bbok-i] a popular, Korean street food of spicy rice cakes, but can also be used as slang for sex (during the woman's period.

땡추 [ddaeng-chu] a monk that drinks, eats meat, picks up girls, plays around and doesn't do his or her job well.

대박이다

[dae-bak-i-da]

score; hit the jackpot; dynamite or stellar

글자상으로, 이것은 큰 박을 의미한다. 한국에서, 특히 20세기 전의 가난한 시대에는 작은 박을 말리거나 삶아서 바가지로 만들었다. 하지만 큰 박으로는 성찬을 즐길 수 있었고, 이를 반영하여 현재는 풍부, 행운, 그리고 좋은 일을 뜻하게 되었다.

Literally "it's a big gourd." During periods of poverty in 19th Century Korea, small gourds were dried and boiled to make dippers, but large gourds could be feasted on, so they came to represent periods of abundance or by reference, great or lucky things. Similar to "wow," "that rocks" or "wonderful," *daebak* is as ubiquitous and overused as "swell" in the 50's, "hip" in the 60's, "groovy" in the 70's, "dope" in the 80's "rad" in the 90's, "phat" in the 2000's, and "epic" since.

여름 제비들 그리고 겨울 박들

옛날 옛날에, 여름과 오빠인 겨울이 살고 있었다. 여동생 여름은 여름 내내 밭에서 열심히 일했고 큰 박들을 길러냈다. 심지어 발을 절뚝이는 제비를 치료해주어 자신의 것처럼 소중히 여기는 착한 아이였다. 오빠 겨울은 여름 내내 사냥을 했고 겨울이 오자, 여름의 수확물을 즐겨 먹었다. 어느날 밤, 아주 큰 겨울 박을 열었을 때 그는 외쳤다. 대박이다, 대박! 그리고는 맛있는 제비찌개를 먹었다.

Summer Swallows and Winter Gourds

Long long ago, there were two siblings, a sister of summer and a brother of winter. The sister, YeoReum, worked hard all summer in the fields, grew grand gourds and even saved a lame swallow, curing it's broken leg and raising it as her own. Brother KyoWul hunted all summer and when winter came, he would enjoy the fruits of the Summer. One night, as he opened a great winter gourd, he said, daebakita, daebak! And ate some delicious swallow stew.

돌아가시겠다

[dol-a-ga-si-get-da]

kill me now; drive me crazy

직역으로는 '내가 죽겠다'는 것을 의미한다. 이것은 '죽겠다'의 존대어로 표현되는 말인데, 여기서는 죽을 정도로 어이없고 어처구니없는 것을 뜻한다.

Literally "to pass away," *dolagasigetda* is used in formal language to refer to a death. As slang, it expresses the feeling of being dumbfounded that comes with an improbable, perplexing or ridiculous situation, invoking feelings associated with a sudden death. Similar to the English expression: "just shoot me!" or "kill me now!"

잃어버린 바지

Mac	무슨 일 있어? 바지는 어쨌어?
PC	딸꾹질(약간의 문제) 때문에 포맷했어.
Mac	그래서 이제는 괜찮아 진거야? 그런데, 네 바지는 어디간거냐구.
PC	아무데서도 찾을 수가 없어! 프로그램도 없어지고 오류메시지 계속 뜨고 바지는 없네. 돌아가시겠다.
Mac	그래, 너 자주 죽을(다운) 때마다 보는 나도 조금씩 죽을 지경이었어.
PC	완전히 돌아가시겠다.

Missing Pants

맥	What happened to you? Where are your pants?
PC	I had the hiccups, so I went in for a reformatting.
맥	So now you are better? But where are your pants?
PC	I can't find them anywhere: programs missing, error messages, and no pants. Dolagasigetda.
맥	Yeah, you die often and I die a little every time I see you.
PC	Absolutely dolagasigetda.

돌싱

[dol-sing]

single and ready to mingle; a divorcée

"돌"은 돌아온, 그리고 "싱"은 싱글의 줄임말로 돌아온 싱글을 의미한다. 이 줄임 표현은 "실패자(Damaged goods)"라는 부정적 의미보다는, "다시 자유"라는 특히 긍정적인 의미를 함축하고 있다. 이 표현은 한국에서의 이혼율 증가와 더불어 이혼에 대한 부정적 태도가 줄어들며 생겨나게 되었다.

Dol (돌) from the Korean *dol-a-un* (돌아온), or returned, and *sing*, (싱) for newly single (돌아온 싱글). This abbreviated expression has a particularly positive connotation of "free again" rather than something negative like "damaged goods." *Dolsing* has come about in recent years with the growing number of divorces in Korea and the lessening of critical attitudes toward divorce.

돌싱반찬의 고백

YuJa	오빠, 나 더 이상은 못 기다리겠어… 언제 프로포즈 할거야?
PaJeon	음, 우선 너한테 한 가지 중요한 얘기 할게 있어.
YuJa	뭔데?! 오빠 엄마가 나 안 좋대?
PaJeon	아니, 아니야! 엄마는 You(Ja), 너를 정말 좋아해…
YuJa	그럼 뭔데?.
PaJeon	어, 나 돌싱이야… 많이 화났지?
YuJa	뭐? 어떤 여자야? 설마 그 매춘부 율무는 아니겠지?!
PaJeon	아니, 아니야… 그녀 이름은 치…. 성은 김씨고.
YuJa	뭐?! 김치와 결혼했었다고? 무슨 일이 있었던 거야?
PaJeon	그냥 쉬어버렸어.

The Straight Scoop

유자 (yu-ja) & 율무 (yul-mu) – YouJa and YulMu are kinds of tea that we have turned into names for the pure purpose of 'hot liquid' personification. 김치 (kim-chi), though not a liquid is hot in it's own way! Rawr Ms. Kim!

Confessions of a Dol-Sing Side Dish

유자	Oppa, I'm not going to be hot forever…
	When are you going to propose?
파전	Well, I have to tell you something important first.
유자	What?! Your mother doesn't like me?
파전	No, no! She loves You(Ja)….
유자	Then what?
파전	Uh, I'm a dolsing… Are you mad?
유자	What? Who was she? Not that harlot YulMu?.
파전	No, no… her name was Chi…. From the Kim clan.
유자	What?! You were married to KimChi? What happened?
파전	It just went sour.

Truncated Terms

The CCEB (Commonly Condensed Expressions Box)

- **깜놀** [ggam-nol] – 깜짝 놀랐다 a sudden shock; a fright

- **돌싱** [dol-sing] – 돌아온 싱글 a return to singledom

- **멘붕** [maen-bong] – 멘탈붕괴 a mental breakdown or collapse (often used by students for stress from excessive studying at test time.)

- **안물** [an-mul] from 안물어봤어 meaning I didn't ask you. So what?

- **엄친아** [eom-chin-ah] from 엄마 친구 아들, literally "my mom's friend's son." This is for highly competitive mothers to compare their child to someone who is good looking, highly successful and rich).

- **행쇼** [haeng sho] from 행복하십쇼, have a good day; don't worry, be happy

돌직구

[dol-jik-ku]

shoot straight; straight talk; be brutally honest

문자 그대로, 돌과 직구의 합성어로 똑바로 던진다는 뜻이다. 돌직구를 하려면 다른 사람의 감정에 대한 고려 없이, 마음에서부터 우러난 솔직한 말을 해야 한다.

Literally "a rock" or *dol* (돌) and "a fastball" or *jik-ku* (직구), to indicate a rock thrown straight and hard. To *doljikku* one must speak bluntly, straight from the heart and without consideration for another's feelings. Similar to "speak frankly," or "don't hold back," it has the sarcastic connotation of "Tell me what you really think!"

Synonym: 솔까말 [sul-gga-mal] to be completely honest; from 솔직히 까놓고 말해서

소개팅 2

ChangHyun	오늘 저 만나서 어땠어요?
Arum	어, 글쎄요…
ChangHyun	괜찮아요… 솔직하게 말해줘요.
Arum	음, 좋은 분 만나셨으면 좋겠어요…
ChangHyun	오… 돌직구.

Blind Date 2

창현	Did you enjoy our date?
아름	Uh, well…
창현	It's OK… tell me what you really think.
아름	Um, why don't you meet a nice girl…
창현	Oh… doljikku.

The Straight Scoop

Blind Date 소개팅 [so-gae-ting] *Sogae* is to introduce someone and the *ting* comes from "meeting" to mean a blind date. See page 185 for more details.

Culturally Speaking

The Cold Hard Truth

In a country as reserved as Korea, sometimes it is refreshing to hear some candor. That is NOT the case here! And frankly speaking, I don't need to hear that I can't dance from you again! No more *doljikku*! Please...

돗대

[doet-dae]

lucky cig; last square

한 개(단위를 셀 때)를 뜻하는 일본어 히토쯔로부터 유래된 단어. 이것이 한국에서는 돗으로 변형되어 단위의 하나인 대와 결합되고, 마지막 담배 한 개피(다른 사람에게 빼앗겨서는 안되는 것)를 의미하게 되었다. 혹은 한국의 당구게임, 4구에서 마지막 포인트를 의미하기도 한다.

From the Japanese *hitotse* meaning "one" (when counting), this was altered to *doet* (돗) in Korean. Then added to the Korean *dae* (대), a marker for counting things. The combination is most often used to refer to a last cigarette (something that should not be given out to or taken by another and sometimes considered lucky) or the last point in a Korean four-ball billiards game.

마지막 한 모금

SiWoo	야 임마, 내 담배 어디갔어? 그거 내 돗대야!
Peter	글쎄, 나한테 그걸 왜 물어? 난 담배 안 피잖아!
SiWoo	잠깐만. 민지 어디 갔어? 그 년! 걔는 맨날 내 담배 빌려가!
	오, 그리고 이제는 담배 살 곳도 없다고!

〔1분뒤〕

Minji	내 귀가 왜이리 간지럽지. 너네 무슨 얘기하고있었어?
Siwoo	담배 하나 빌려가는건 괜찮아, 하지만 그냥 가져가는거는 다르잖아!
	그건 내 돗대였다고!
Minji	뭐? 나 저번달에 담배 끊었잖아! 너 분명히 네가 피워놓고
	까먹은거야! 이 골초야!
Siwoo	(흐느끼며) 나의 돗대, 나의 예쁜 돗대 어디간거야?

One Last Puff

시우	Hey man, where are my cigarettes? That was my doetdae!
피터	Well, what are you looking at me for? I don't even smoke!
시우	Wait a minute. Where is Minji? That bitch! She's always bumming cigarettes! Oh, and there's no place to buy them now!

[1 minute later]

민지	My ears are itchy. What were you talking about?
시우	Bumming a cigarette is one thing, but taking them is something else! It was my doetdae!
민지	What? I quit smoking last month! You must have smoked it and forgot! You golcho!
시우	(Whimpering) My doetdae, where's my pretty doetdae?

The Straight Scoop

내 귀가 왜이리 간지럽지 "My ears are itchy." When someone is talking about you in your absence, your ears are said to be itchy. In America, your ears are said to 'burn' in such a case.

됐거든(요)

[duet-geo-deun(yeo)]

forget-about-it; yeah, whatever

글자 그대로, 그것으로 충분해 혹은 됐습니다의 짧은 표현이다. 친한 친구들 사이에서만 사용되며 요즘은 이것을 더 짧게, 됐것으로 종종 이야기한다.

Literally, an abbreviation of the expression for "that's enough" or "that's OK," *dueseubnida* (됐습니다), and only used between friends. This phrase is closely related to the English expressions "don't say another word," "give it up," "shut the fuck up" or "forget-about-it," and is and may be accompanied by a hand to the face to show that you are tired of hearing someone's bullshit excuses. *Duetgeodeun* can also be shortened further to *duetgot* (됐것).

전화 벨

ChangHyun	아름아, 방금 전화하려던 참이였어.
Arum	됐거든! 너 몇주동안 전화한통 없었어! 그날 밤 이후로.
ChangHyun	난, 음... 중간고사 때문에 바빴어.
Arum	됐거든요! 너 절대 공부 안 하잖아! 그리고 너 빅터랑 룸살롱 간 거 다 들었어.
ChangHyun	누가 그래? 나 절대...
Arum	됐어. 우린 끝났어!! 그럼... 됐것!

Phone Ringing

창현	Arum, I was just about to call you.
아름	Duetgeodeun! You haven't called me in weeks! Not since that night.
창현	I, um... I've been busy with midterms.
아름	Duetgeodeunyo! You never study! And I heard you were with Victor at that room salon.
창현	Says who? I never...
아름	Duesseo. We're finished!! Then... duetgeot!

된장녀

[duen-jang-nyo]

material girl; gold digger

영어표현 shit 또는 damn과 비슷한 의미를 가지고 있는 단어, 젠장으로부터 변형된 말이다. 이 표현은 이와같이 발음상의 유사점 때문에, 그리고 배설물의 색과 된장의 색이 비슷하듯, 머리속에 똥이 찬건지 된장이 찬건지 구분 못 할 정도로 물질적 가치만 따르는 여성을 일컫는 말이 되었다.

Taken from the word *jaenjang*, an expletive similar to "shit" or "damn," this expression changed to *duenjang* (soybean paste), which also sounds similar and has the color of excrement. Distantly related to the expression "material girl," it describes a woman who is willing to live on only *duenjang* stew in order to afford designer handbags or shoes, but also carries the connotation of a shallow woman who is only after material wealth (a gold digger looking good for a sugar-daddy to marry).

PC의 복수

Mac	야, 나 방금 압구정 다녀왔어. 여자들 전부 예쁘더라.
PC	그렇긴 해도 걔네들 거의 다 된장녀야.
Mac	뭐? 냄새가 된장같다고, 아님 된장을 먹는다고? 상관없어!
PC	아니, 걔네는 명품에만 관심있다고. 이기적이고 사치스러워.
Mac	된장녀가 누군지 어떻게 구별해?
PC	iPad 들고 다니는거 보면 딱 알 수 있어.

PC's Revenge

맥	Man, I just went to Apkujeong. The girls are all beautiful.
PC	Yeah maybe, but most are duenjangnyo.
맥	What? They smell like duenjang, or eat duenjang? I don't care!
PC	No, they just care about material things. Selfish and conceited.
맥	How do I know which ones are duenjangnyo?
PC	The iPads are a sure giveaway.

뒤땅까다

[dui-ddang-gga-da]

to bitch about someone; talk trash; talk shit

뒤땅의 의미는 한국의 전통 민속게임 윷놀이로부터 유래하였다. 이것은 윷놀이에서, 상대
편의 말이 다 앞선 뒤의 뒤쫓고 있는 다른 말들을 의미한다. 이것이 까다의 때리다라는 의
미와 결합되면서 누군가를 뒤에서 욕하는 것을 뜻하게 되었다.

The meaning of *duiddang* comes from the traditional Korean game of *yut*, in which it
means to be among the group trailing the lead horse. When combined with the
hitting aspect of *ggada*, it has come to mean speaking ill of someone. Similar to the
English expressions "talk behind somebody's back," "trash talk" or "talk shit about
someone," and relates to a gossip monger.

Synonyms: 뒷담 [dui-dam] & 뒷담화 [dui-dam-hwa] gossip (literally "back wall talk"), 뒷
담화까다 [duid-dam-hwa-gga-da] say spiteful things (literally, behind someone's head).

선두주자

DaeJung   절대 안돼! 또 다른 박이 대선후보 당선이야?

         근혜가 과보를 잇게 되었어. 때로는 업보가 세대를 뛰어넘기도 하지.

YoungSam   넌 뒤땅까는 것 좀 자제해. 난 네가 뒤땅이었던 때를 기억하고 있어.

         그리고난뒤 세력을 다시 잡은거잖아…

DaeJung   네가 맞다. 우리 김씨들이 본보기가 되어야지.

The Front Runner

대중   Another Park in office? Never! GeunHye got what she deserved.
Sometimes Karma skips a generation.

영삼   Maybe you shouldn't duiddang-ggada so much. I remember
when you were the duiddang. And you came back to take the
lead again…

대중   You're right. We Kims need to lead by example.

뒷북치다

[duit-buk-chi-da]

old news; yester-say

글자 그대로는 북의 뒷면을 치다. 비속어로 이것은 이미 끝난 일(끝난 이야기)에 수선을 떠는 것을 의미한다. 이 표현은 타이밍과 관련된 것으로 이와 비슷한 영어표현으로는 that's old news 가 있다.

Literally "to hit the backside of the drum." Here, *duitbuk chida* means to make a fuss about something that is already finished (or has already been hashed out). Timing is everything with this expression and it relates to the American expressions "that's old news," "give it up," "stop beating a dead horse" or "thanks for the history lesson."

밝고 밝은 어느 화창한 날

DooHwan 대중이 소식 들었지? 노벨평화상 탔대!

SeungMan 응. 드디어, 우리 대한민국의 꿈이 이루어진거야.

DooHwan 와우, 대중이가 우리나라를 위해 정말 많은 일을 했구나.

〔5분 후, 대중이가 웃으면서 걸어온다〕

DaeJung 화창한 날이다. 그지? 내가 무슨 일하고 왔는지 들었어?

SeungMan 뒷북치네. 뒷북. 자랑 그만해라.

DooHwan 허! 전과자 주제에 잘난척 하기는.

A Bright, Bright Sunshiny Day

두환 Did you hear about DaeJung?
He just won the Nobel Peace Prize!

승만 Finally, our dreams of a Great Korean Empire are coming true.

두환 Wow, he's done so much for our country.

[5 minutes later, DaeJung walks in smiling]

대중 It's a bright day isn't it? Did you hear what I did?

승만 Duitbukchida. Duitbuk. Quit bragging.

두환 Huh! Ex-con trying to make himself out to be better than others.

따 (왕따, 은따, 전따)

[dda (wang-dda, eun-dda, jeon-dda)]

a black sheep; a loser, loner or reject

그룹 내에서 심하게 따돌림을 당하거나 외면 당하는 사람을 의미하는 말이다. 특히 학교에서 주로 사용되는 표현. 따는 여러가지 조합으로 사용되어지는데, 가장 일반적인것은 왕따, 반에서 가장 소외당하는 학생을 의미한다. 은따는 그들 스스로 인기있다고 생각하지만 실제로는 은근히 따돌림 당하고 있는 학생을 의미하고, 전따는 교내 전체에서 가장 따돌림 받는 아이를 말한다.

Someone who is shunned, ostracized or excluded from a group, especially in a school setting. *Dda* can be used in several combinations, the most common is *wangdda* [literally "king outcast"] for the most shunned student in a class; *Eundda* ["secretively outcast"] refers to someone who thinks they are popular, but are widely disliked; and *jeondda* ["total outcast"] the biggest pariah in the entire school.

Also: 루저 [ru-jeo] a loser (mostly about appearance); esthetically challenged

은에서 금으로

Mac	빌, 너 왕따지, 아니야? 내가 너 빵셔틀 당하는거 봤어.
PC	좆까! 난 공부 잘해서 애들이 좋아해!
Mac	하하. 그러면 너 은따겠지.
PC	진짜래도 스티브, 나 인기도 많고 똑똑하잖아.
Mac	내가 따일수도 있지만, 넌 진짜 전따야.
Teacher	Gates! Jobs! 따 새끼들, 체육수업으로 돌아가 안그러면 머리박는다.

Silver to Gold

맥	Bill, you're a wangdda, aren't you? I saw you have been doing the bread shuttle.
PC	Hell no! I'm admired for my good grades!
맥	Ha ha. Then you must be an eundda.
PC	Really Steve, I'm popular and smart.
맥	Maybe I'm a dda too, but you really are a chundda.
선생님	Gates! Jobs! You dda SOBs get back to gym class or else you'll be on your heads.

Corporal Punishment

The Serious Suffering of School Sanctions

Corporal punishment was still commonplace in schools and the military in Korea until recently. It is becoming less and less acceptable, though it is still used upon occasion to discipline students.

- **머리박다** [meor-i-bak-da] Literally "to beat your head." Originally from the military, *meoribakda* is a form of punishment where you put your head on the ground with your arms behind your back and your legs spread to form a tripod. Teachers will make delinquent male students assume this acutely uncomfortable, painful position as a potent reminder to obey. A prime example can be seen in the movie *Chingu* (친구). Thanks Teach!!

Other forms of punishment

- **손 들기** [son deul-gi] standing with one's arms raised (also a common punishment of young children by their parents).

- **오리 걸음** [or-i gyeor-eum] walking like a duck.

- **앉았다 일어나기** [anj-at-da il-eo-na-da] doing (an excessive amount of) squats.

- **책으로 학생 머리 때리기** [chaeg-eu-ro hak-saeng meo-ri ddae-ri-gi] hitting a student's head with a book. OUCH!

따가리

[dda-ga-ri]

a lighter; a bic

라이터를 켤때 생기는 마찰의 소리(딱 딱 딱)로부터 유래되어 현재는 그 자체(라이터)를 의미하는 비속어가되었다.

Probably originating from the clicking sound made when thumbing a lighter (*Ddak ddak ddak*), this onomatopoeic word became slang for a lighter.

이리와 내사랑 내 가슴에 불을 지펴줘

Siwoo	불 있어?
Peter	뭐? 원시인처럼?
Siwoo	아니, 따가리 있냐고.
Peter	그 빌어먹을 따가리가 뭔데?
Siwoo	임마, 라이터! 라이터! 속어로 라이터야!
Peter	그럼, 왜 그렇게 말 안했어? 좆나, 영어좀 배워, 짜샤.
Siwoo	넌 한국말 좀 배워, 개새! 그래서... 가지고 있어?
Peter	좆까 없어! 그리고 넌 담배좀 끊어! 골초!

Come on Baby Light My Fire

시우	Do you have fire?
피터	What like a caveman?
시우	No, do you have a ddagari?
피터	What the fuck is a ddagari?
시우	A lighter man! A lighter! It's slang for a lighter!
피터	Well, why didn't you say so? Learn some fucking English, man.
시우	You learn some Korean, bitch! So... do you have one?
피터	Hell no! And maybe you should quit smoking! Golcho!

따먹다
[dda-meok-da]

to have a one-night stand; taste one's fruit; get some

보통 과일을 먹는 것을 연상시키는 표현. 하지만 여기서 이 속어는 하룻밤 즐기며 관계를 갖는 사람들에게 사용되어진다. 또한 따는 강제적, 일방적인 의미를 기초적으로 내재하고 있다.

Literally meaning "to pick and eat" (as in a piece of fruit), here it is used for a person, as in to have a one-night stand. *Dda* (따) involves the idea of the biblical forbidden fruit as well as an element of force or coercion in many cases. Similar expressions in English are to "bag," "tag" or "score with" (a girl), or even to "get a piece."

줄리아나 과일안주

PaRam	형, 어디 갔었어? 과일 다 없어졌어.
SunSu	윗층. 호텔에... 그 영계 따먹었어.
PaRam	벌써? 정말 선수라니깐! 여자를 좀 소중히 여겨야 할텐데.
SunSu	형이 신선한 복숭아 좀 먹었다고 지금 질투하는구나.
PaRam	에이 싸가지없다!

Juliana Fruit Plate

바람	Hyeong, where have you been? The fruit's all gone.
선수	Upstairs. At the hotel... I ddameokotda that chick.
바람	Already? You're such a player! You should have more respect for women.
선수	You're just jealous 'cause I had a fresh peach.
바람	Such an ass!

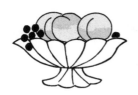

딱지 떼다

[ddak-ji ddaeda]

to pop one's cherry; lose one's virginity

글자 그대로 풀이하면, "상처의 딱지 따위를 떼어내다"의 의미. 이것은 불법 주차를 하였을 경우, "주차구역이 아닌 곳에 주차하였을 때" 주로 쓰이는 표현이다. 하지만, 비속어로 이 단어는 남자가 처음 여자와 관계를 맺은 것을 뜻하며, 아주 가끔의 경우에 여자에게 사용된다.

Literally to "take off" or "peel off" (*ddaeda*) a "scab" (*ddakji*), this rather nasty expression is often used for removing a parking ticket sticker meaning, "Parking in a no parking zone." The slang, however refers to the first time a man has had sexual intercourse, thereby "becoming experienced" or "popping his cherry." This expression is rarely used when referring to a woman.

주차중

ChangHyun	어젯밤, 결국 아름이를 러브모텔에 데려갔어.
TaeYong	너 딱지 뗸거야? 축하해.
ChangHyun	뭐? 그건 축하 할 일이 아니잖아.
TaeYong	너 처음 한거지. 아니야?
ChangHyun	...딱지 뗸거? 아니야. 나 맨날 불법주차해.
TaeYong	아, 너 'parking ticket' 끊은거야? 모든 모텔에는 주차창이 있을텐데.
ChangHyun	술집 앞에 차를 데고 갔거든.

Parking the Car

창현	Last night, I finally took Arum to a love motel.
태용	You got a ddakji ddaeda? Congratulations.
창현	What? That's not anything to congratulate me on.
태용	It was your first time. Wasn't it?
창현	...to get a ddakji ddaeda? No. I always park in the wrong place.
태용	Oh, you got a 'parking ticket'? But every motel has a parking lot.
창현	I left the car in front of the bar.

Sex Box

Sense and Sexuality

- 섹스 [sek-se] sex (borrowed from English / ubiquitous)
- 하다 [ha-da] to do it (have sex)
- 자다 [ja-da] to sleep with (have sex)
- 몸을 섞다 [moem-eul-seogg-da] to mix bodies (have sexual intercourse)
- 성관계 [seong-gwan-gae] to have sexual relations (more of a medical term)
- 떡을 치다 [ddeok-eul chi-da] hitting rice caked (like slapping uglies)
- 혼전성관계 [hon-jeon seong-gwan-gae] to have premarital sex
- 성교 [seong-gyo] intercourse (coitus or sexual congress)
- 합궁 [hap-geung] having sex (archaic, a bit like "making house")
- (성욕을) 자극하다 [seong-yuk-eul ja-geug-ha-da] - arouse sexual desire
- 섹스숍 [sek-se-shop] or 포르노점(店) [po-re-no-jeom] a place to buy those awesome toys or little nightie-nothings
- 딸딸이 [ddal-ddal-i] masturbating (childish) for a bit of fun on your own. [most often used specifically for public masturbation]
- 자위하다 [ja-ui-ha-da] beat off or jack off
- 수음을 하다 [su-eom-eul ha-da] to play with oneself (also a hand job)
- 사까시 [sa-gga-si] oral sex or a blowjob (from the Japanese)
- 구강 성교 [gu-gang seong-gyo] fellatio or cunnilingus
- 빠구리 [bba-gu-rl] buggery or doggy style ass-fucking
- 보지 [bo-ji] muff or pussy (slang for a vulva and related to a flower)
- 자지 [ja-ji] the penis (slang equivalent to the English cock or dick)
- 물건 [mul-geon] literally, a thing (slang for the penis)
- 좃털 [jot-teol] a man's pubic hair (literally "cock fur"),
- 잡털 [jab-teol] a man's pubic hair (literally "impure fur")
- 보지털 [bo-ji-tol] a woman's pubic hair (literally "pussy fur")
- 떡볶이 [ddeok-bogg-i] magic sex (during the woman's period)
- 라볶이 [ra-bogg-i] magic pubes (red pubic hair that results from having sex during the woman's period)
- 걸레 [geol-lae] an easy woman (literally, a rag)
- 갈보 [gal-bo] a prostitute, a whore

땡땡이 치다

[ddaeng-ddaeng-i chi-da]

to play hooky; skip school

글자 그대로는 종을 친다는 뜻이지만, 땡땡이 치다는 반드시 해야하는 작업을 하지 않은 채 게으름을 피우고 노는것을 의미한다. 이것은 학교 수업을 빼먹고 도망치는 경우에 자주 사용된다. 하지만 일과 작업을 끝내지 않고 피하는 모든경우에 사용되어질 수 있다.

Literally, to strike a bell. To *ddaengddaengi chida* is to avoid some work that must be done. It is most often used for skipping school, but can be used for procrastinating on a project or skipping work as well. Equivalent to the English expressions: "play hooky," "ditch school" or "cut class."

고담시티 땡땡이

Robin	배트맨, 가자! 리들러가 시청을 점령했대.
Batman	별로, 흥미없어.
Robin	뭐야 땡땡이 치는거야?
Batman	나 오늘 휴일이야. 그리고 비키 만나러 가야해.
Robin	비키도 거기있어. 납치당했다고!
Batman	음, 땡땡이 그만쳐 임마! 빨리 출발하자.

Gotham City Bells

로빈	Let's go, Batman! The Riddler has taken over City Hall.
배트맨	Nah, I'm not interested.
로빈	Why are you ddaengddaengi chida?
배트맨	It's my day off. And I'm going to see Vicki Vale.
로빈	She's there too, she's been kidnapped.
배트맨	Well, stop ddaengddaengi chida and let's go.

땡잡다

[ddaeng-jab-ta]

to grab some luck; catch a lucky break

간단히, 땡은 행운이나 운수를 의미하고 잡다는 쥐어 가지는 것을 의미하여 운이 좋은 것을 의미한다. 비슷한 영어표현으로는 'hit the jackpot' 또는 'make a killing.'이 있다.

Simply speaking, *jabta* is to grab and *ddaeng* is good fortune or a lucky break. Similar expressions in English are to "hit the jackpot" or "make a killing."

좋은소식 까치

Ggachi	뭐!! 왜 계속 째려봐?
Jaebi	어서 얘기해! 인터넷에서 봤는데, 지저귀는 까치를 보면 좋은 일이 생기고 귀한 손님이 온댔어. 나 땡잡고 싶어.
Ggachi	그래서 어쩌라고… 그건 그냥 미신이야.
Jaebi	나 나중에 소개팅도 있는데 영계도 만나고 싶어서.
Ggachi	그놈의 여자타령! 땡잡고 싶으면, 새들을 쫓아다니지 말고 나무가 되어야겠지?

The Good News Magpie

까치	What?! Why are you just staring at me?
제비	Start chatting! I read on the Internet that a chatting magpie brings good news and welcome guests. I need to ddaengjabta.
까치	So… that's just a superstition.
제비	Well, I have a sogaetting later and I need to meet a hot chick.
까치	You and your birds! If you want to ddaengjabta, why don't you stop chasing birds and just be the tree?

띠껍다

[ddi-ggeob-da]

to sneer at someone; to act bitchy or catty

마음에 안 드는 무엇인가를 표현할 때 사용된다. 특히 누군가의 얼굴표정이나 태도가 마음에 안 들때 자주 쓰이며 매스꺼울정도로 마음에 들지 않음을 나타내는 역겹다라는 표현과 비슷하다.

Used to describe something disliked particularly someone's snide facial expression or bitchy attitude. Possibly related to *yeokgyubda* (역겹다), meaning nauseating or revolting. Distantly related to the English expressions: "wipe that grin off your face," and "what the fuck are you looking at?"

그 웨이터

MinHee   나 너무 배고파. 그 느려터진 웨이터 어디갔어?

HeeYeon   그리고 걔 너무 띠꺼웠어. 예의도 없고! 어떻게 조지지?

Arum   아, 왜그래. 그냥 냅둬. 일하는게 너무 힘들어서 그런 걸 수도 있잖아. 그냥 기분좋게 먹자.

MinHee   안돼. 띠꺼워. 걔는 내가 얼마나 이쁜지 모르는거야? 어떻게 그런 못생긴 얼굴을 나한테 보일 수가 있어?

Waiter   식사 나왔습니다. 숙녀분들을 오래 기다리게 해서 죄송해요. 후식은 무료제공이구요. 그럼 식사 맛있게 하세요.

The Waiter

민희   I'm so hungry. Where is that waiter? He's so slow.

희연   And he was so ddiggeopda. No respect! How dare he!

아름   Awe, come on. Give the guy a break. Maybe he's just having a rough day. Let's enjoy the meal.

민희   No, he was really ddiggeopda. Doesn't he know how pretty I am? How can he show me such an ugly face?!

웨이터   Here's your food ladies, so sorry for the delay. And the dessert is on the house. Enjoy your meal.

Riul's Absence is a Mystery

Neither an R nor an L in sight.
What happened to riul's ㄹ might?
Initial R or L when final,
riul's ㄹ absence is a mystery,
missing in the pages of this book's history.
Few words begin with its ㄹㄹㄹ rolling sound
So skip to mium ㅁ and have another round..

Two Lips Meet
to Merge Complete

Like two lips separating soundly
Making a mandible of mium ㅁ roundly.
Mumbling a mantra as it stared
into the madness of the storm squared.
Ma-ma-ma 마마마 from the 마음 ma-eum
of heart, of home.

만먹다

[man-meok-da]

to give lip; not show respect to elders

이 비속어는 필적하다라는 의미를 가지며 정확히 만먹다라고 발음되는 맞먹다라는 표현으로부터 유래되었다. 이 비속어는 만만히라는 단어에서 전해진 만이라는 단어와 너의 말을 먹는다, 혹은 존칭어를 떼겠다라는 먹다라는 단어와 결합되어 반말하며 존댓말을 사용하지 않는것을 의미하게 되었다.

The meaning comes from the expression, *matmeokda* (맞먹다) meaning to be equal, which is actually pronounced *manmeokda*. When combined with *man* (만) from *manmanhee* (만만히) meaning negligently or slightingly, and to eat from *meokda* (먹다) as in eating your words or leaving off a polite ending, this indicates using disrespectful language.

예의 위반

ChangHyun	야 피터, 요즘어때? 잘 나가?
Peter	야? 너 지금 나랑 만먹자는거냐?
	이리와. 내가 예의가 뭔지 가르쳐줄게.
ChangHyun	넌 나 못잡잖아! 바보!
Peter	이 쪼끄만 새끼! 잡히면 나한테 궁뎅이 쳐 맞을줄 알아!

A Breach of Protocol

창현	Ya Peter, 'sup? How they hangin'?
피터	Ya? You trying to manmeokda me?
	Come here and I'll teach you some manners!
창현	You can't catch me! You fool!
피터	You little shit! I'm gonna kick your ass!

말리다

[mal-li-da]

to dry up; not go well; botched or jacked up

건조시키다, 못하게하다, 혹은 말다(내가 돌돌 말려서 아무것도 못하게 되듯)라는 단어로부터 유래되었다. 이는 무엇인가가 잘 진행되지 않을 때, 무언가 망쳤을 때, 혹은 어떠한 것에 리듬감을 잃고 헤맬 때 사용하는 비속어이다.

Literally "to dry out" or "to prohibit" (Another possible origin is from *malda* (말다) meaning to roll something up, as in "I'm all rolled up and can't do anything right"). *Mallida* can be used to describe something not going well, some failing, to lose one's rhythm, or to ruin something.

마른 날

Peter	오늘 플레이가 잘 안돼?
Bom	어, 전부 말린다.
Peter	왜? 또 무슨 일 있어?
Bom	어제는 아들 생일인데 사장이 늦게까지 붙잡는 바람에 아들 얼굴도 못보고 마누라는 그것 때문에 나랑 얘기도 안해. 어제부터 말리네.
Peter	괜찮아질거야. 긍정적으로 생각해. 적어도 비는 안오겠지.

A Dry Day

피터	Can't play ball today?
봄	Yeah, I'm all mallida.
피터	What's wrong?
봄	Yesterday, my boss wouldn't let me go till late, so missed my son's birthday party. Now, my wife won't talk to me. The whole day is malinae.
피터	It'll be all right. Look on the bright side. At least it's not raining.

말 까다

[mal gga-da]

speak plainly; dispense with the niceties

"고상함 없이, 걸치레 없이 이야기 한다"는 의미. 직역으로 이것은 "반말" 또는 낮춤말 한다는 것을 의미한다. 반말은 친구들이나 자신보다 어린 사람들과의 사이같은 비형식적인 상황에서 사용되어진다.

Literally "to peel away (dispense with) the niceties" and "to speak plainly or without pretense." Essentially, *mal ggada* means "to speak *banmal*" (the Korean low, familiar or informal language) when it is not appropriate to do so. *Banmal* can be used in informal situations among friends or with people younger than you, but should not be used to superiors, elders or anyone not close to you.

용산에서

MinShik	당신도 용띠였네요!
JiTae	당근이지.
MinShik	와우, 전 그쪽이 형인줄 알고 있었어요! 지금부터 그냥 말까자.
JiTae	말까지마 이런... 그래도 내가 너보다 생일이 2달 빠르잖아.

On Dragon Mountain

민식	You are from the year of the dragon too!
지태	Of course.
민식	Wow, I always thought you were a hyeong! Let's just mal ggada from now on.
지태	Don't mal ggada, you cad. Even so, my birthday is two months before yours!

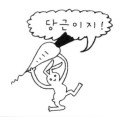

The Straight Scoop

당근이지 [dang-geun-i-ji] literally "it's a carrot," *Danggeun* means "obviously" "you bet" or "no shit!" This expression comes close in sound to the Korean *tangyeonhaji* (당연하지) meaning "of course." [Also, *muloniji* (물론이지)]

This then evolved into 말밥이지 [mal-bab-i-ji], literally meaning, "it's horse food," from the concept that a carrot is horse food. However, in the late 90's, I heard the expression 물개이지 [mul-gae-i-ji] short for 물론이지 개새끼야 [mul-lon-i-ji gae-sae-ki-ya] or "of course, you son of a bitch." This last expression is much less common and some Koreans have never even heard it, but it's fun to use and explain to them anyway. Somewhat similar to the English expression "Does a bear shit in the woods?" or better yet, "No shit, Sherlock!"

Also, there is the simple and sweet 콜 [kol] used ubiquitously to answer questions in the affirmative, meaning "sure" "you bet" or "certainly."

당빠지 [dang-bba-ji] or 당삼빠따지 [dang-sam-bba-dda-ji] are other fun ways of saying *tangyeonhaji* (당연하지), maybe somehow related to three carrot bats(?), but more importantly, these expressions are preferred for their sound than their derivation and may be purely onomatopoeic in origin.

형 [hyeong] literally means an older brother, but in Korean can be used by any man for another older man as a term of respect.

이런 [i-reon] literally meaning "such a..." or "this kind of..." It implies an ending of a swear word or something less powerful, like a cad.

맛이 갔다

[mash-i-kat-da]

went crazy; lost one's senses; in a tizzy

음식의 맛이 가다(쉬다)의 의미에서 변형되어 사용되어졌다. 음식이 쉬는 것처럼 사람의
정신이 온전하지 못하게 되었을때 이르는 말, 또는 술을 많이 마셔 이성을 잃은 사람에게
사용한다.

As with food that has gone bad, *mashikatda* indicates a person who has lost control
of his or her senses either from being crazy, or (more commonly) from drinking too
much. Similar to "lose one's cool," or "lose one's shit!"

프랑스 레스토랑

ByungShik 주방장 왜저래? 광성이는 갑자기 왜 때린거야.

HwaSeok   맛이 갔어. 광성이가 뭐라고 한 마디 하니까 이성을 잃어버렸어.

ByungShik 이런, 접시까지 집어 던지고 있네! 도대체 주방장한테 뭐라고 한거야?

KwangSung 난 그저 달팽이 요리 맛이 갔다고 했지.

HwaSeok   맛이 갔다고 했다고? 너 방금 미쳤다고 한거네.

The French Bistro

병식   What's wrong with that chef? He just attacked KwangSung.

화석   Mashi gatda. KwangSung said something and the chef just
      lost it…

병식   My god, he's throwing dishes! What did you say to him?

광성   I just told him that the escargot had gone bad.

화석   You said mashi gatda? You just called him crazy!

맞장뜨다
[mat-jang-ddeu-da]

go toe-to-toe or face off (with); mano-a-mano

일대 일의 의미를 가지고 있는 맞이라는 단어와, 우두머리와 대장을 뜻하는 장이라는 단어, 결정하다라는 의미를 함축하고 있는 뜨다라는 단어가 결합되어 싸우자는 것을 의미하는 비속어이다. 보통 중,고등학생들이 많이 사용한다.

Literally, *mat* (맞) meaning face-to-face and *ddeuda* (뜨다) to bestow [in a sense to decide on] the title of *jang* (장) which is a head, leader or chief. To *matjangddeuda* is to face off against one's opponent, engaging in hand-to-hand combat to see who is the better man or to settle a score. Usually used by middle or high school students, and similar to "go toe-to-toe with someone" or the commonly used Spanish expression for fighting man-to-man, "mano-a-mano."

복수전

ChangHyun	병식아. 우리 둘 뿐이다. 너 계급장 떼고 맞장뜨고 싶지?
HwaSeok	네?
ChangHyun	내가 기억하기로는 나를 대장 농땡이라고 했던것 같은데?
	한번 싸워보자.
HwaSeok	아닙니다. 전 절대 대장님과 싸울 수 없습니다.
ChangHyun	너 커피 한 잔이면 다 끝난줄 알았지?
	나보고 귀차니스트 농땡이라며.
	그래, 지금은 안 귀찮으니까 싸우자. 주먹 쥐고 손 올려.

Settling the score

창현	OK, ByungShik. We're all alone now.
	You want to forget rank and matjangddeuda.
화석	Sir?
창현	As I recall, you called me Corporal Nongddaengi,
	didn't you? Let's see what you're made of.
화석	No Sir. I can't fight you.
창현	You thought the coffee was the end of it? Guichanist
	nongddaengi, you said. Well, I'm not lazy now,
	so get your idle hands up...

몰카(지)

[mol-ka-ji]

(am I being) punk'd

이 축약어는 한국 TV쇼 이경규의 몰래카메라에서 유래되었으나 연출되었거나 비현실적으로 보이는 어느 상황에서나 사용하게 되었다. 미국의 TV쇼 Candid Camera와 Punk'd 사이의 느낌이다.

Literally "it's a hidden camera, isn't it." This shortened expression meaning "something's not right here" (said in response to a prank) is derived from a TV show in Korea named *GyeongGyu Lee's Hidden Camera*. It has come to be used for any situation that seems staged or surreal and is less old-school Candid Camera, and more the Ashton Kutcher style Punk'd show.

꿈 속의 한 장면

〔번잡한 카페에 들어서며〕

PC 어서 자리 잡아서 저 맥빠들에게 내 멋진 새 PC 자랑하고 싶다!

〔주위를 둘러본다.〕

PC 어, 다들 윈도우를 사용하잖아! 잠깐, 이거 몰카지? 어디 구석에 Mac이 숨어있는 거 아냐? … 없어, 없잖아! 여긴 천국이야, 드디어 우리가 이겼어! 음냐…

Mac 일어나, 일어나! 네가 어젯밤 조각모음하고 재설치 하느라 밤샌 거 아는데, 그래도 카페에서 자면 안되지.

〔PC 잠에서 깨 모든 테이블에 있는 Mac, 아이패드, 아이폰을 본다.〕

PC 뭐? 심지어 몰카도 아니야? 카메라 없어? 그냥 맥들뿐? 차라리 몰카에 당하는 게 낫지!

108

The Dream Sequence

[walks into a crowded coffee shop]

PC   Can't wait to get settled in and show off my snazzy new PC to all those silly Mac fans.

[looks around]

PC   Uh, everyone is using windows! Wait, this is molkaji?! Is Mac lurking in some corner?… Nope, nowhere! I'm in heaven, finally we've won! Mmmmm.

Mac   Wake up, wake up! I know you spent all night defragging and reinstalling, but you can't sleep at a coffee shop.

[PC wakes up to see Macs, iPads and iPhones on every table]

PC   What? It's not even a molka? No cameras? Just more Macs! I'd rather be punk'd!

Culturally Speaking

Koreans love taking pictures, of themselves, of their food, of themselves with their food. The selfies can get a bit excessive. I once watched a young lady taking selfies on the subway… In an hour plus train ride, she had still not gotten the shot quite right. She never stopped!

More Camera Slang

몰카 [mul-ka] (몰래 카메라) [mul-lae ka-mae-ra] a hidden camera

디카 [di-ka] (디지털카메라) [di-ji-teol ka-mae-ra] a digital camera

셀카 [sael-ka] (셀프 카메라) [sael-peu ka-mae-ra] a selfie

셀카봉 [sael-ka-bong] (셀프 카메라 봉) [self camera bong] a selfie stick

엽사 [yeob-sa] (엽기 사진) [yeob-ki sa-jin] a silly photo

먹방 [meok-bang] (먹는 방송) [meog-neun bang-song] food program (or pics)

물이 좋다

[mul-i joh-ta]

the water is good; it's hoppin'

글자 그대로는 수질이 좋다라는 뜻이지만, 이 표현은 나이트클럽이나 파티와 같은 특정한 장소에 잘생기고 예쁜 남,여가 많음을 의미한다. 이와 관련있는 영어 표현으로는 There are many fish in the ocean.이 있다. 질문 형식으로 물이 어때라는 표현이 자주 쓰이고, 반대 표현으로는 물이 구리다라는 표현이 사용된다.

The literal meaning of "the water is good" infers that there are fish in the water or that the scene at a particular nightclub, party, or other venue is good as it is full of attractive or available men or women. Related to the English expressions "there are many fish in the sea" or "come on in, the water's fine."
In question form 물이 어때 [mul-i eo-ddae] how's the water, is often asked, and if the water is not good, its opposite is 물이 구리다 [mul-i gu-ri-da] the water is gross.

물 밖의 고기

HaPum   명태야 벌써 파티갔어? 물이 어때?

MyongTae   끝내주지. 물 완전 좋아. 빨리 오렴!

[1시간 후...]

HaPum   뭐야? 물 좋다고 했잖아... 완전 물 구리다...

SaengTae   너희가 빨리 왔어야지. 우린 둘다 여자 번호 땄지롱!

MyongTae   그래, 사람 완전 많았는데 술 떨어져서 다들 나가버렸어.

                 이젠 물이 구린게 아니라 아예 물이 없다.

HanSum   귀여운 남자들은 다 어디갔지? 지겹고 마실것도 없고.

                 물 밖 고기 신세된 기분이야.

SaengTae   그럼 물 좋은데로 가자.

HaPum   아, 그 물좋다는 물 나이트 가자는 소리구나!

A Fish Out of Water

하품   Hey MyungTae, are you at the party yet? Muli oddae?

명태   Yeah, it's great. Muli johta. We're doing booking… Hurry up!

[1 hour later…]

하품   What happened? This party sucks. Absolutely, muli gurida. You said the party was good…

생태   You should have come earlier, we both got girls' numbers!

명태   Yeah, it was full of people, but everyone left when the liquor ran out. Now, worse than muli gurida, there isn't any water at all… Absolutely muli obta.

한숨   Where did all the cute guys go? I'm bored and there's nothing to drink. I feel like a fish out of water!

생태   So let's go where the water is good.

하품   You mean Mool – the mul johta nightclub!

몽땅

[mong-ddang]

all-in; everything; completely

이 표현은 '모두'의 충청도 지방 사투리에서 유래되었다. 그러나 또한 욕망, 탐욕을 의미하는 '몽'이라는 단어와 지구 혹은 대지를 뜻하는 '땅'이라는 단어가 결합되어 모든것을 의미하기도 한다. (또한 짧고 굵은것을 뜻할때도 쓰이는데 '몽땅연필'을 예로 들 수 있다.)

This slang expression is most likely derived from the Chungchong province dialect for *modeu* (모두), meaning everything. However, we suggest that it could also come from the combination of *mong* (몽), meaning greed, with *ddang* (땅), referring to the Earth or the land, to communicate the concept of everything, similar to "the whole enchilada" or in the case of gambling, "I'm all-in."
(*Mongddang* can also be used for something short and fat, like a stubby pencil.)

다다익선

JiTae   너 도박 왜 계속 하는거야? 돈도 이제 거의 없잖아.

MinShik   난 몽땅 가지던지, 몽땅 잃던지 화끈한게 좋아.

JiTae   하지만 식구들은 어떡해.

MinShik   어짜피 마누라도 펑펑 쓰는걸 뭐. 마누라는 몽땅걸,

그리고 나는 몽땅가이야…

The More the Better

지태   Why are you gambling? You hardly have any money left.

민식   I want to get mongdang or lose mongddang.

지태   But what about your family?

민식   My wife will spend it all either way.

She's a mongddang girl and I'm a mongddang guy…

Babbling Biup, Buzzing Free

A bit like the B of bat and ball,
and free to fall from puckered lips,
P pursed then softly parted
Abuzz with bees' abundance
back and forth ㅂㅂㅂ, the buzzing started.
Beware the biup, but speak free...
B666 is indubitably the letter for me.

바가지 긁다

[ba-ga-ji geulk-da]

to nag someone; to bitch and moan

문맥적으로, 박을 긁다라는 뜻. 이것은 부인의 듣기 싫은 불평(보통, 금전적인 부분에 대한 불평)을 반영하는 비속어이다. 한국에서 바가지는 전통적으로 국자와 같은 용도로 사용되었다. 또한 이는 조선시대 거지들이 밥을 구걸할 때 사용되기도 하였다. 바가지 긁는 것은 빈 바가지를 긁는 것이다. 그 소리는 영어식으로는 칠판 긁는 소리와 비슷하다고 할 수 있다.

Literally "to scrape the gourd." This expression refers to the annoying sound of a nagging wife (usually in reference to getting, earning or making money). Gourds are traditionally used as ladles in Korea, but they were also used by beggars in the Joseon Dynasty, beating it to beg for rice. A scraped gourd is an empty gourd. The sound loosely relates to the English concept of scraping the chalkboard.

반쯤 비어있는 박

Ajumma1	요즘 어때?
Ajumma2	우리 남편 승진했어. KFC에서 파티할거야.
Ajumma1	좋~겠네... 우리남편은 한 번도 승진한적 없는데.
Ajumma2	네 남편은 의사잖아! 승진할 수가 없지. 너 남편 바가지 긁니?
Ajumma1	나 열쇠 3개 가지고 시집왔어. 난 불평할 권리 있다고.
Ajumma2	더 이상 뭘 원하는건데? 우리는 아무것도 없이 시작했지만, 난 바가지 긁은적 없어. 난 사랑을 위해 결혼했고, KFC면 만족해.
Ajumma1	사랑이 밥먹여 주니? 넌 반 쯤 빈 바가지에 행복할지 몰라도 난 더 원해.

The Gourd is Half Empty

아줌마1   How're things?

아줌마2   My husband got a promotion. We're celebrating at KFC.

아줌마1   That's great... I guess. Mine never gets promoted.

아줌마2   He's a doctor! He can't be promoted.
Do you bagaji geulkda?

아줌마1   Well, I came with three keys, so I can complain if I want.

아줌마2   What more do you want? We started with nothing and
I never did bagaji geulkda. I married for love and
I'm happy with KFC.

아줌마1   Love won't put food on the table. Maybe you're happy with a half
empty gourd, but I want more.

Culturally Speaking

Three Keys

열쇠 3개 [yeol-sue sae-gae] Traditionally, a doctor or lawyer in Korean
culture is so sought after as a husband that a woman who wishes to marry
one is often expected to bring three keys to the marriage: one for a new
car, an office (for his practice) and a house.

밤새 달려

[bam-sae dal-ryeo]

to party hardy; run all night; stay up drinking

문자 그대로는 "밤새 동안 달리자"는 의미로, 영어표현 "let loose" 혹은 "run rampant" 와 비슷하다. 이는 술로 밤을 지새우며 신나게 노는 것에 대한 표현이다. 주로 대학생들이 나 직장인들이 술을 거하게 한 잔 하자는 요청을 할 때, 이 표현을 사용한다.

Literally "let's run all night" and similar to the English sayings "let loose" or "run rampant," this expression is about having an unrestrained night of drinking that rages through the night. Often used by college students or office workers as a call to let loose and get excessively drunk.

D는 "달려"

Bill	야 테드. Mr. Ryan이 과학점수 D 줬어!
Ted	훌륭하네! 우리 밤새 달려야겠다!
Bill	안돼, 임마… 나 너무 피곤해.
Ted	뭐? 파티 안 한다고? 너 패스했잖아!
Bill	오늘 체육수업에서 Mr. Kim이 계속 운동장 돌게 했거든. 난 더 뛸 수가 없다.
Ted	아니 빌. 내 말은, 파티 하자고… 밤새 달려!
Bill	좋았어 친구! 파티를 시작하자!

D is for Dalryeo

빌	Hey, Ted. Mr. Ryan just gave me a D, in science class!
테드	Excellent! We should bamsae dalryeo!
빌	No, man… I'm too tired.
테드	What? No party? But you passed!
빌	I had gym class today and Mr. Kim made me run laps all day. I just can't run any more.
테드	No Bill. I meant, let's party… bamsae dalryeo!
빌	All right dude! Party on!

바가지 쓰다
[ba-ga-ji sseu-da]

to get ripped off; pay a lot for crap

문맥적으로, 바가지를 머리에 뒤집어 씀을 의미한다. 비속어로는 구매시 불필요하게 많은 비용을 지불했을 경우 사용되며, 빈 바가지를 들고 다니는 거지와 같이 될 것이다 혹은 어디에도 사용될 수 없는 그 바가지를 머리에나 써라는 뜻을 내포하고 있다.

Literally "to put a gourd on your head," and meaning that if you pay too much for something useless, you will soon become like a beggar with an empty gourd and nothing more to do with it than put it on your head.

원형통 현찰

SeungMan 왜 바가지를 쓰고 다녀?

DaeJung 뭐? 나 그런적 한 번도 없어.

SeungMan 그럼 나보고 네가 했던 햇볕정책을 성공적이었다고 믿으란 말이야?
 회담 한답시고 얼마를 북에다가 갖다 바친거야?

DaeJung 너와는 상관 없는 일이야.

SeungMan 완전 바가지 썼어.

DaeJung 무의미했던 일 아니야! 난 노벨상을 받았다고!

Cash on the Barrel

승만 Why did you bagaji sseuda?

대중 What? I never did anything of the sort!

승만 I guess your Sunshine Policy was a success then?
 How much did you pay the North to come to the bargaining table?

대중 That's none of your business.

승만 Really bagaji sseuda.

대중 It wasn't for nothing! I got the Nobel Prize!

반사

[baŋ-sa]

right back at you; ditto

언어적 공격을 당했을때 어린이들이 주로 사용하는 비속어 표현이다. 이와 관련된 영어표현으로 "나는 고무, 너는 풀, 너가 뭐라고 나에게 말하던 이건 다시 너에게 붙어버릴거야." 라는 표현이 있다.

Literally meaning "reflection" and used by children in response to some verbal attack, it is similar to the childish English expressions "no backs," or "I'm rubber and you're glue, whatever you say bounces off me and sticks to you."

외모와 지성

YeoReum   오빠는 못생겼어!

KyoWul   반사! 너는 무식하잖아!

YeoReum   더블 반사!! 어 그래, 나는 무식해도 공부해서 똑똑해지면 되지만 오빠 평생 못생긴 얼굴로 살아야되잖아!

KyoWul   이거 왜이래. 내가 원하면 엄마가 성형수술 시켜준댔어!

Brawn and Brains

여름   You're ugly!

겨울   Bansa! And you're stupid!

여름   Double bansa!! Oh yeah, I can study and get smarter, but you'll always be ugly!

겨울   What are you talking about? Mom says I can get plastic surgery if I want!

방콕

[bang-kok]

staycation (vacation in your room); stay home

벌이 쏘면 침이 계속 박혀있듯, 방에 콕 박혀있을 것이라는 의미. 이 표현은 공부, 일에 지친 학생(직장인)들이 그들의 쉬고싶은 마음을 표현하기 위해, 혹은 그들의 스트레스로부터 벗어나고 싶은 마음에 사용하는 비속어이다…또는 휴가 동안에 할 일이 없거나 갈 곳이 없는 사람들을 위한 변명이기도 하다.

Literally "to sting (콕) the room (방)." When a bee stings something, it is stuck there for good. This expression is used by worn-out students (or workers) to describe their desire to rest or get away from everyday stress… they can also say this as an excuse for having nothing to do or nowhere to go.

전망 좋은 방

Peter   겨울방학때 뭐할거야?

SiWoo   방콕할거야.

Peter   와우, 좋겠다! 뱅콕 너무 좋아!
거기가면 성들 전부 구경하고 타이 마사지는 꼭 받아야해!
PatPong 지역은 엄청 위험하니까 가지 말고.

SiWoo   아니, 그 뱅콕 말고 방콕! 내 방에서 자고 쉴거라고.

Peter   임마, 재미없잖아! 뱅콕 가자! (노래 부르며)
"뱅콕에서의 하룻밤은 거만한 남자도 겸손하게 만든다."

A Room with a View

피터   What are you going to do for winter vacation?

시우   I'm going to bangkok.

피터   Wow, cool! I love Bangkok! You've got to see all the palaces
and definitely get a Thai massage while you're there!
But avoid PatPong; it's really dangerous!

시우   No, not Bangkok, bangkok. I'm going to stay in my room
and sleep.

피터   Man, you're boring! Let's go to Bangkok! (Starts singing)
"One night in Bangkok makes a hard man humble."

배째라

[bae-jjae-ra]

I'd rather die; my mind is made up

글자 그대로는, 나의 배를 갈라라. 이는 어쩌면 할복자살을 의미하는 일본어 셉뿌꾸로부터 유래된 것일지도 모르겠다. 누군가 막무가내로 행동할때, 혹은 문제를 해결할 의지가 없을 때 쓰인다.

Literally "cut my stomach." *Baejjaera* is used to describe one's own stubbornness or unwillingness to alter a position to the death, which may come from the Japanese for committing *seppuku* – a ritual suicide, cutting the stomach. It can also mean, "what's done is done" and loosely relates to the Shakespearian expression "take a pound of flesh" or the line from Guys and Dolls: "so sue me, sue me, shoot bullets through me…"

일파운드의 살점

JiTae	민식. 여기 공평한 제안을 가져왔다.
MinShik	이 집, 너에게 팔 수 없다고 이미 말했을텐데. 배째라.
JiTae	언젠가 너와 똑같이 말했던 놈이 하나 있었지.
	나에게 돈을 빌려가놓고는 배째라며, 돈 없다고 하더군.
MinShik	그래서…
JiTae	그래서 쨌지.
MinShik	그럼 넌 더이상 돈을 받을 길이 없겠구나! 하 하! 멍청이!

A Pound of Flesh

지태	MinShik. I made a fair offer for your house.
민식	I'm not going to sell it to you and that's final. Baejjaera.
지태	I had a guy say the same thing to me the other day.
	He owed me some money, and when I asked,
	he said he didn't have it. Baejjaera, he said.
민식	So…
지태	So I did.
민식	And now you can never get the money! Ha ha! Idiot!

100m 미인

[baek-mi-teo mi-in]

good from far, but far from good; butt-ugly or fugly

"멀리서는 좋지만 좋은것으로부터는 멀다," 라는 영어식 표현과 비슷하다. 누군가 멀리 떨어져 있을 때 외모가 예쁨을 이르는 말로, 가까이 있을 때는 아름다움과 거리가 먼 사람을 일컫는 말이다. 특히 화장을 두껍게 하는 여성을 말한다.

Literally "a 100-meter beauty." Similar to the English expression "good from far but far from good" and related to a "two-o'clock beauty queen," *100m mi-in* suggests that someone may appear pretty from a long way off, but up close is far from beautiful. This also applies to "beer goggles" when drunk and is particularly common for girls who hide behind thick makeup.

화면보호기

Mac   야 PC, 너 쫓아다니는 여자 아니야? 예쁘다!

PC   후지쓰? 멀리 있으니까 그렇게 보이는거야.

         저여자 100m 미인이야.

Mac   뭐? 외롭다고 맨날 불평했잖아. 무조건 데이트 해야지.

PC   아니라니까! 화면보호기(화장) 하지 않은 저여자 보기 싫어!

Mac   그건 술 취하면 해결되는거고.

PC   그럼 아침에는?

Mac   아, 그렇구나. 네가 무슨 말 하는건지 이제야 알겠다…

Screensaver

맥   Hey PC, isn't that the girl who's always chasing you?
      She's pretty!

PC   Fujitsu? You just think so 'cause she's far away.
      She's a 100m mi-in.

맥   What? You always complain that you're lonely. You should date her.

PC   No way! I don't want to see her without her screensaver (makeup).

맥   But that can easily be solved by a good pair of beer goggles.

PC   And in the morning?

맥   Oh, I see what you mean…

볼매

[bol-mae]

to grow on someone

"볼수록 매력있다"의 줄임말로, 계속 볼수록 더 나아지는 것이나 사람을 설명하는 말이다. 처음에는 인지하지 못했지만 어떤 사람을 점점 더 매력적으로 보이게 하는 설명할 수 없는 무언가를 말한다.

Short for *bol-su-rok mae-ruck eet-da* (볼 수록 매력있다), it describes something or someone that looks better, the more you see them. That indescribable attribute of someone that seems to grow on you, making them seem more and more attractive despite initially being overlooked.

볼매 되기

MinJi	걔가 희연이 새 남친이라고? 농담이지?!
MinHee	그래그래, 걔가 잘생기진 않았지만 설명할 수 없는 무언가가 있다고…
	내 생각에 아마 걔는 볼매인 것 같아.
MinJi	오, 그럼 돈이 많나? 운 좋은 기지배.
MinHee	돈도 없어. 품격이 있을 뿐.
MinJi	뭐라고? 잘생기지도 않고 돈도 없어? 도대체 어디서부터 시작해야 돼?
MinHee	어쨌든. 바로 그게 볼매잖아.
MinJi	성격이 좋나보네.. 네 말이 맞나보다.

Being Bolmae

민지	He's HeeYeon's new boyfriend?! You've got to be kidding!
민희	OK, OK, he's not much to look at, but he's got that *je ne sais quoi*, that pleasant quality that's hard to describe; that indescribable something… I guess he's bol-mae.
민지	Oh, so he has money?! That lucky girl.
민희	No money, just class.
민지	What? No looks and no money? There's nothing to even start with?
민희	Whatever. That's what bol-mae is!
민지	Full of personality, I guess… I'll have to take your word for it.

불금

[bul-geum]

TGIF; burning Friday night

모든 사람들이 주말을 좋아하지만, 최근 몇 년까지만 해도 토요일마다 자주 일했던 한국인들은 특히 주말을 사랑한다. 영어 TGIF와 비슷한 의미로, 이는 불타는 금요일의 줄임말이다. 많은 한국인들이 그들의 친구들 혹은 직장 동료들과 술자리를 즐기는 것만큼 술은 진탕 마셔야 하며, 얼굴 또한 살짝 빨개지는 것이 기본이다.

Everybody likes weekends, especially Koreans who until recent years would often have to work on Saturday's. Similar to the English "TGIF," it is short for *bul-ta-neun geum-yo-il* (불타는 금요일), or literally "burning Friday." And as many Koreans enjoy going out for drinks with friends or coworkers, it also has to do with "painting the town red," and maybe getting a little red faced from drinking too much as well.

불에 타다

Mac	와, 불금이다!
PC	어, 그래. 특별한 계획이라도 있는 거야?
Mac	물론이지. 모든 "i"들과 도심을 떠나 스키타러 갈거야. 넌?
PC	하드드라이브가 맛이 가서 주말 내내 다시 포멧하고 디프레그 해야 해.
Mac	흠, 걱정마. 끝내주게 재미있는 동영상을 우리가 만들고 편집해서 보내줄 테니까.
PC	불금은 개뿔… 사무실을 다 태워버리든지 해야지!

Getting Burned

맥	Waaa, it's bulgeum!
PC	Uhhh, yeah. You've got big plans?
맥	Yeah, out on the town tonight. Then going skiing with all the **i**'s. What about you?
PC	My hard drive is fried so I've got to spend the whole weekend reformatting and defragging.
맥	Hmmm, don't worry. We'll make, edit and post a fabulous video of all the fun for you.
PC	Bulgeum, my ass… I should burn the office down!

벼락치기
[byeo-rak-chi-gi]

wing it; off the cuff; on the fly

글자 그대로 번개를 뜻한다. 무슨 일이 임박해서야 준비하는것을 보고 일컫는 말로, 특히 학생들이 시험보기 전, 마지막 순간에 할 때 주로 사용된다.

Literally "a thunderbolt." This expression is used to describe some hasty preparation, especially with regard to studying at the last minute, or as we say in English: "cram" or "pull an all-nighter."

공부 거의 하지않기

Bill 벌써 기말고사 기간이네?! 짜식, 공부는 했냐?

Ted 어! 사실, 안했어. 우리 시험 잘 봐야하는데.
안그러면 Mr. Ryan이 우리 F줄거야. 벼락치기가 필요해.

Bill 어떻게 하면 학교에 벼락을 만들 수 있을까?…
아 그래. 시험 직전에 과학실에서 폭발을 일으키면 되잖아.

Ted 그럼 Ryan은 시험 취소할거고. 즐겨보자!

Bill 벼락치기없는 벼락. 훌륭해.

To Study Hardly

빌 It's final exam week already?! Dude, did you study?

테드 Way! Well, actually no. We need to have a triumphant test or Mr. Ryan is going to fail us. We need a byeorakchigi.

빌 How can we get a thunderbolt in the school?… I know. We could create an explosion in science class just before the exam.

테드 And Ryan would cancel the test. Party on!

빌 A thunderbolt without the byeorakchigi. Excellent!

불알친구

[bul-al chin-gu]

childhood friend; bosom buddies; BFF

이 표현은, 서로 벌거벗은 모습 봐도 어색하지 않을 정도로 어릴적 부터 친구였던 사이를 일컫는 표현이다. (나쁜 표현은 아니다.)

Literally "ball friend" or "testicle friend," *bulal chingu* merely refers to a friend from early childhood, one that was so young as to have seen the other in the unabashed nudity of infancy. (Not considered vulgar.)

잘 달고 다녀?

Kaeul	우리 공주님이 벌써 이렇게 컸어… 첫번째 데이트도 한다고 하고.
Bom	창현이랑 간다지? 칫. 여름이 불알친구.
Kaeul	귀여운 불알 좀 만져보자며 고놈 불렀던게 엊그제 같은데.
Bom	우리 여름이 건들면, 그녀석 불알 콱 터뜨려버리겠어!

How they hangin'?

가을	Our little girl is growing up… She's going on her first date.
봄	And with ChangHyun. Ts. Her bulalchingu.
가을	I remember when I used to call him over to grab his little balls.
봄	And if he touches her, I'll have his balls in my hand!

The Straight Scoop

불알 좀 만져보자 [bul-al jeom man-jyeo-bo-ja] grab his little balls. In Korea, parents or grandparents often think it's cute to see or even handle a young boys balls (in a non-sexual way) until age 4-5. This practice is fading due to enhanced awareness of sexual abuse at least in the major cities.

125

불타는 고구마

[bul-ta-neun go-gu-ma]

lit up; blitzed or blotto; red-faced drunk

글자 그대로 해석하면 불타고 있는 고구마를 뜻한다. 이 비속어는 누군가 술을 너무 마셔 그 얼굴이 고구마와 같은 색깔로 변했을 때 사용된다(특히 한국에는 이렇듯 알콜에 알레르기를 가지고있는 사람들이 많다).

Literally "a blazing sweet potato." *Bultaneun goguma* refers to someone who has had so much to drink (read – fire water) that their face has turned the color of a sweet potato. Koreans are particularly susceptible to this problem as many are allergic to alcohol, yet they go, go, go!. (Think, drunk as a skunk!)

백수 집합

〔편의주 하면서〕

Minji   아, 저 거지 돈 달라고 또 왔어.

Migu   냄새도 완전 구리고, 얼굴도 불타는 고구마네.

Minjii   너도야! 너도 만만치않게 얼굴 시뻘게. 얼마나 마셨냐?

Migu   한 병 밖에 안 마셨어. 근데 민지야, 너도 거지잖아.

내 말은 너도 지금 백수라고. 안그래? 소주 더 먹고 싶으면 너가 저 사람한테 돈 달라고 해야지. ㅋㅋ.

Minji   백수 아니야. 난 백조지.

Migu   (혼잣말로.) 백사겠지.

빨리 취직해야지. 안그러면 너도 저렇게 돼.

Minji   우리가 술을 그만 마시던지 같이 더 퍼 마시던지 해야겠다!

Migu   그래그럼, 너 돈 있으니까 저 사람 소주 사주고 우리 모두 불타는 고구마 친구하자.

The Straight Scoop

편의주 [pyeon-ui-ju] a combination of 편의점 and 맥주 or 소주 and meaning to meet someone for a beer or a smattering of soju on the plastic chairs outside a convenience store (most commonly in nice Spring/Fall weather).

The BaekSu Crew

[out for PyunuiJu]

민지   Oh my, here comes that beggar again. Trying to ask for money.

미구   He smells so bad and he looks like a bultaneun goguma.

민지   So do you! You're as red-faced as he is. How much did you drink?

미구   Just one bottle. But Minji, you're a beggar, I mean baeksu now too, aren't you? You should ask him for money for more soju. Kh kh.

민지   I'm not a baeksu, I'm a baekjo.

미구   (Under his breath.) More like a baeksa. You'll end up a beggar too, if you don't get a job soon.

민지   Either we should stop drinking or we should all have some more!

미구   Well, you've got money, so let's buy him some soju and all become bultaneun goguma friends.

The Beggar Box

Unemployed, Unemployable or Utterly Indolent

거지 [geo-ji] a street beggar, but not the only kind in Korea...

"Not a beggar, but a bum." These expressions all refer to someone with no job or nothing to do. Basically a lazy person with money to burn.

- 백수 [baek-su] Literally "white hand," a *baeksu* is an idler who does nothing, has no job and really isn't even looking for work. They are getting their money from some unknown source, usually their parents.

- 백조 [baek-jo] Literally "white swan," a female *baeksu* is usually a young beautiful girl that doesn't need to work (or is just unemployed and loafing).

- 백사 [baek-sa] Literally "white snake," is a treacherous or wicked girl that pretends to be a *baeksu*. A *baeksa* is actually working in some capacity where she is taking a bite out of men, maybe as a room salon girl.

- 꽃뱀 [ggot-baem] Literally "flower snake," similar to a white snake (*baeksa*).

- 백여시 [baek-yeo-su] A "white fox" is a crafty and capricious woman.

- 이태백 [ee-tae-baek] 20대 태반이 백수, 20-somethings stuck without a job because of the bad economy and living off their parents.

- 취집 [chui-jib] a woman who deliberately seeks to become a housewife.

불어

[bul-eo]

tell all; spill (it)

문자 그대로는 트럼펫따위를 불다, 혹은 휘파람을 불다라는 뜻. 비속어로는 아는 것 전부 를 말하다, 혹은 비밀을 감추지 않고 다 말하다를 의미한다.

Literally "to blow" (as with a trumpet) or "whistle." As slang *buleo* means to "tell all" or "keep no secrets," and has the same connotation as the English expression "spill one's guts."

랄프 로렌

SoYoon	오늘 한 남자가 우리 사무실에 왔었어.
	뉴욕에서 온 패션가이였는데...
JiYoon	패션?! 불어. 이름이 뭔데? 회사는!
	너 내가 얼마나 패션을 사랑하는지 알잖아.
SoYoon	랄프 거시기래나 뭐래나...
JiYoon	랄프 로렌! 그사람 내 우상이야! 어서 불어. 그남자 어때 보였어?
	그 사람이 뭐래? 옷은 뭘 입었디? 그사람 폰번호는 뭐야?!
	불어. 불어. 불어.

Ralph Lauren

소윤	A guy came to my office today. Some fashion guy from New York...
지윤	FASHION?! Buleo. What's his name? What company! You know how I love fashion.
소윤	I think it was Ralph something...
지윤	Ralph Lauren! He's my idol! Quickly Buleo. How did he look? What did he say? What was he wearing? What's his phone number?! Buleo. Buleo. Buleo.

빈대불다
[bin-dae-but-da]

to be a parasite or freeloader; to mooch; sponge from

글자 그대로 빈대가 달라붙는 것. 빈대가 몰래 달라붙어 숙주의 피를 빨아먹는것처럼, 이 표현은 누군가 요금(보통 식사비 또는 유흥비)에 대한 공정한 지불을 하지 않을 때 사용된다.

Literally "a bedbug clinging." As a bedbug secretly clings to its host to suck its blood, this refers to someone not contributing a fair share to a fee (for food or entertainment), and to leech or "sponge off" of someone.

다른 곳에 선행 베풀기

WonDong	야, 민지가 어떻게 도망쳤지? 또 당했어.
DongWon	돈 안내고 도망칠 작정이었어! 걔는 맨날 빈대붙네.
WonDong	왜 우리는 항상 빈대붙게 놔두지?
DongWon	그래도 민지는 재있는 빈대니까.
WonDong	그런 선행을 다른 곳에 좀 베풀면 좋으련만. 민지한테 문자보내자.
DongWon	"푹 자! 빈대가 물게 냅두지 말고."

Pay it Forward

원동	Man, how did she do that? Minji strikes again.
동원	She managed to get away without paying! She's always bindaebutda.
원동	Why do we always let her bindaebutda?
동원	I guess it's 'cause she's such a fun bedbug.
원동	I hope she at least pays it forward. Let's send her a text.
동원	"Sleep tight! Don't let the bedbugs bite."

~빠

[~bba]

a follower; a fan or groupie

한국의 어린 소녀패들은 종종 "오빠"라고 소리를 지르며 유명한 가수나 배우들을 쫓아다녔기 때문에 오빠와 순이의 합성어인 빠순이라고 불리게 되었다. 십대 팬들은 지나치는 경우가 있으므로 빠순이의 줄임말인 "~빠"는 지나치게 무언가에 빠져있는 사람을 가리킨다. 유명한 사람, 정치인이나 심지어 브랜드 등과 같이 쓰일 수 있다.

Young female fans in Korea would often chase popular K-Pop Idol singers or famous actors while screaming "*oppa~~~~*!!!!" (older brother), so these girls became called *bba-sun-i* 빠순이 (a combination of 오빠+순이). Teenage fans can be over the top, so the shortened form of *~bba* describes someone who's excessively into something with the name of that thing or person preceding it. It can be used for famous people, political figures or even brands.

과일 대 곡식

YulMu	세상에, 살이 엄청 찌네. 거기다 추석도 금방이고! 나 어떡하지?
YuJa	너 구석기 다이어트 한 번 해봐.
YulMu	잠깐, 그거 곡식 안 먹는 거 아냐?
YuJa	당연하지. 빵은 나쁘다구! 너 곡식이 너한테 얼마나 나쁜지 몰라? 난 분명 시트론빠야.
YulMu	그치만 난 보리빠데. 젠장, 난 보리로 만들어졌잖아.
YuJa	그래서 너가 그렇게 뚱뚱한가 보다.
YulMu	그리고 너 남자친구가 파전 아니야?
YuJa	아마 우리 잠깐 서로에게서 시간을 가져야 할까봐.

Fruit vs. Grain

율무	Oh my god, I'm getting so fat and Chuseok is coming up! What am I going to do?
유자	You should try the Paleo diet.
율무	Wait. Isn't that where there's no grain?
유자	Of course. Bread is bad! Didn't you know how bad grain is for you? I'm definitely citron~bba.
율무	But I'm barley~bba. Heck, I'm made of barley.
유자	Maybe that's why you're so fat.
율무	And isn't your boyfriend Pajeon?
유자	Maybe I need a break from Pajeon for a while.

빡세다

[bbak-soe-da]

to go grey (from hard work); to get the life sucked from you

글자그대로는 머리가 회색으로, 하얗게 혹은 창백해진 것을 의미한다. '빡'은 누군가의 머리를 낮춰 이르는 말로서 정중한 대화에서 사용해서는 안되는 표현이며, '세다'는 힘든 일로인해 머리카락이 하얗게 변한 것을 뜻한다.

Literally "to make your head turn grey, white or even pale." *Bbak* (빡) is a low expression for someone's head so this should not be used in polite conversation, and *soeda* (세다) means to turn white, ostensibly from hard work.

최종 기한

Siwoo 여기 앉아서, 너랑 책 쓰는 일은 빡세.

Peter 그래, 나도 알아. 25살도 안됐는데 벌써 머리가 샜어.

Siwoo 장난하냐? 뭐야, 나 흰머리 있냐?

Peter 하! 그냥 농담이야! 너 낚였지! ㅋㅋ 니 얼굴 창백해 지는걸 봤어야 하는데!

Siwoo 창백한 얼굴? 너가 백인이잖아... 내가 이렇게 책쓰는 일을 통해 얻는 것이라고는 단지, '빡세다! 빡세다!' 뿐이야.

The Deadline

시우 Sitting here working with you on this book is bbaksoeda.

피터 Yeah, I can tell. You're already getting grey and you're not even 25.

시우 You're joking?! Oh no, I have grey hair?

피터 Ha! Just kidding! I really had you going, didn't I! Kh kh. You should have seen your face turn pale!

시우 Pale face? You're the white one... That's all I'll ever get from writing this book! Just Bbaksoeda! Bbaksoeda!

빠돌다

[bbak-dol-da]

blow one's top; go ballistic; wig out; go ape shit

누군가의 머리가 회전하는 것. 이 비속어는 누군가 머리가 회전할 정도로 화나는 일이 있을 때 적합한 표현이다. 또한 이 표현은 폭발을 비유할 때 종종 쓰이는 의성어 '팍'으로부터 변형된 '빡'과 미쳐버리는 것을 의미하는 '돌다'와의 결합형태로 추측해 볼 수도 있다.

Literally "to turn, rotate or spin one's head." This would be best described as one's head spinning from being so angry. *Bbak* (빡) may also be related to the onomatopoeic Korean word for an explosion, *pak* (팍), and *dolda* (돌다) could be to go crazy as in the childish Korean expression to describe someone as crazy, *dorai* (돌아이).
Synonym: 빡치다 [bbak-chi-da] lose one's temper.

열난 빡을 위한 비타민 C

YuJa	나 열 나. 너무 열 나.
PaJeon	뭐? 또 열받은거야? 이번엔 뭣땜에 그래? 날 정말 미치게 하는구나.
	정말 빡돈다! 날 차라리 기름에 튀겨라!
YuJa	아니, 나 아파, 열이 높아서. 머리가 끓고있어.
Pajeon	오, 자기야 미안... 따뜻한 유자차 한잔 마시는게 좋겠어.

Vitamin C for a Hot Head

유자	I have a fever. I'm piping hot.
파전	What?! You're angry again? What is it this time?
	You're making me crazy. Really bbakdolda!
	Why don't you just burn me in oil?!
유자	No, I'm sick, with a high fever. My head is boiling.
파전	Oh, sorry honey ... You should drink some YuJa tea.

Feeling Box

"Wo, Wo, Wo, Feel-ings"

Levels of Happiness

좋다 – 좋앙 – 완전 좋앙 – 죽을 것 같아

- **기분이 좋다** [gi-bun-i jot-da] feeling good, feeling fine
- **신나다** [shin-na-da] elated
- **재밌다** [jae-mit-da] interesting or fun
- **즐겁다** [jeul-geop-da] merry, cheerful
- **행복하다** [haeng-bog-ha-da] just plain happy

Levels of Anger

짜증나다 – 짱나다 – 짜잉나 – 열나짬뽕나

- **삐지다** [bbi-ji-da] to be sulky or cross
- **성나다** [seong-na-da] get angry
- **빡치다** [bbak-chi-da] lose one's temper.
- **열받다** [yeol-bad-da] literally "I'm getting a fever," and meaning to be steaming with anger.
- **좆같다** [jot-kat-da] literally "like a dick," and meaning "This is fuckin' terrible!"
- **짜증나다** [jja-jeung-na-da] meaning to be irritated or annoyed with someone, or to be about to lose one's temper.
- **화나다** [hwa-na-da] anger, simple and sweet
- **게거품 물다** [gae-go-pum mul-da] to foam at the mouth (bite a crab's foam)

Somewhere in Between

웃프다 – 안습

- **웃프다** [oot-peu-da] abbreviated from the Korean for laughter and sadness, it describes something that is funny and sad at the same time
- **안습** [an-seup] so sad (and ridiculous) as to make you cry

뽀대난다

[bbo-dae-nan-da]

cool; the shit; the cat's meow

폼을 의미하는 단어 '뽀다구'와 흘러나옴의 의미를 가지고 있는 '나다'가 결합되어 멋있는 것을 뜻하는 비속어가 되었다. 이 표현은 마돈나의 "strike a pose" 의 인기로부터 유래된 것 같다.

Probably stemming from *bbodagu* (뽀다구), to strike a pose, and *nanda* (난다), to come out, to form new slang for cool, hip or glamorous. It seems to have come into existence during the Madonna "strike a pose" craze. So sexy and stylish aren't you Mr. Fancy pants!

화려한 물고기 포즈

MyongTae   한숨이 봤어? 걔 완전 뽀대났었는데.

SaengTae   걔가 뭐? 지금 모델이라도 하고있어?

MyongTae   아니, 그냥 멋있어보였다고... 한숨이 뽀대나잖아.

SaengTae   내 생각엔 네가 걔를 좋아하는 것 같은데. 혹시 알아?

           네가 'strike a pose'라도 하면 걔가 널 주의깊게 봐줄지.

A Fancy Fish Photo Shoot

명태   Did you see HanSum? She was bbodaenanda.

생태   She what? She's modeling now?

명태   No, she just looks cool... She's bbodaenanda.

생태   I think you've got a thing for her.
      You should "strike a pose" when you see her and
      maybe she'll notice you.

뽀록

[bbo-rok]

pure luck or dumb luck

때때로, 우리는 제비뽑기의 운을 바래야 할 때가 있다… 그래서 우리는 이렇게 말한다: 국어에서 "뽀록나다"는 속어로 '들통나다'의 의미로 쓰인다. '뽀록'은 일본어 '보로'에서 온 말로 파생적의미 '허술한'의 뜻이다. 어쩌면 이 표현은 영어표현 "but luck."으로부터 온 표현이라고.(어쨌든 이는 그저 행운을 의미한다.)

Every once in a while, we have to grasp at straws… so here we go: The dictionary meaning is to be caught in a lie, as in "a lie is detected" or has "come out." Which is originally from the Japanese for humble or shabby. However, we believe the slang usage is derived from English, similar to "but luck" (I know just a stab in the dark, but the sources tell us it means "pure luck" or simply "dumb luck").

럭키 스트라이크

Victor	그거 봤어? 창현이 안타쳤어.
Peter	에이, 걔 그냥 눈감고 방망이 휘두른거야! 그거 뽀록이야.
ChangHyun	아니야. 난 스타야! 넌 삼진 아웃!
Peter	두번째 타석에서는 아웃당했잖아.
Victor	초짜의 운보다 좋은건 없지. 뽀록 야구.

Lucky Strike

빅터	Did you see that? ChangHyun got a base hit.
피터	Hell, he just closed his eyes and swung! That's bborok.
창현	No it's not, I'm a star! You struck out!
피터	You were out at second!
빅터	Nothing better than beginners luck. Baseball bborok.

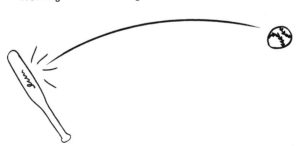

뽀리다

[bbo-ri-da]

to shoplift; a five-finger discount

이 표현의 기원은 찾지 못했다. 다시한번 제비뽑기 식의 발상으로 생각한다면, 어쩌면 이는 borrow(물어보지 않고 빌리다)라는 영어로부터 전해진 것일지 모르겠다. 보로우 = 뽀리? 혹은 "보리, 보리, 쌀." 이라는 한국의 놀이로부터 온 표현일지도. 어쨌든 이는 가게에서 물건을 훔치는 것을 의미한다.

We can find no known origin of this expression. Maybe, it's from the English for "to borrow without asking," borrow = *bbori*? Again with the straws... or from the Korean game, "*bori, bori, ssal*," where a child must grab the fist of someone when they say rice (*ssal*), but not when they say barley (*bori*) – which might be considered theft. Anyway, it means to shoplift.

제인의 중독

Siwoo	야 피터, 이 Jane's Addiction의 노래내용이 뭐야?
	"...내가 무엇인가를 원할 때. 그리고 지불하기는 원치않을때.
	난 바로 문으로 걸어간다... 그리고 바로 문으로 걸어간다."
Peter	물어보지않고 빌려가는것에 대한거야... 훔치는거. 해본적 있어?
Siwoo	아, 뽀리는거. 그럼, 당연하지. 다들 하는거 아니야?

Jane's Addiction

시우	Hey Peter, what is this Jane's Addiction song about?
	"...When I want something and I don't want to pay for it. I walk right through the door... and I walk right through the door."
피터	It's about borrowing without asking... Shoplifting. Have you?
시우	Oh, you mean bborida. Yeah, hasn't everybody?

뽕브라

[bbong-beu-ra]

padded bra; false advertising

여자의 음부를 뜻하는 저속한 표현 뽕으로부터 유래된 표현. 아마도 한달의 일정기간 동안 밑깔개를 대야하는 사실 때문에, (교양없는 소리하여 죄송합니다만, 사실로 보여집니다) 그리고 브라라는 단어와 합쳐져 한국어화 되었다.

From the low expression for the female genitalia (*bbong*), possibly due to the fact that part of the month, it must at certain times be padded (sorry, it sounds so crass but it appears to be true) and the Koreanization of the word bra.

남자 젖

TaeYong	봉아, 너 무슨일 있던거야?
WonDong	맞아, 너 뽕브라 입은것처럼 보여.
TaeYong	그래, 네 이름하고도 어울린다. 봉이 뽕브라를 입고있다.
WonDong	매일 Kraze Burger만 먹었어? 너 젖 생겼어!
Bong	꺼져!

Man Breasts

태용	Hey Bong, what happened to you?
원동	Yeah, you look like you're wearing a bbongbeura.
태용	Yeah, it even matches your name. Bong wearing a bbongbeura.
원동	You been eating Kraze Burger every day? You've got man breasts!
봉	Fuck off!

뽕빼다

[bbong-bbae-da]

get your money's worth

글자 그대로 해석하면, 보지를 빼다. 여자의 음부를 저속히 이르는 뽕이라는 단어와 꺼내는것을 의미하는 빼다라는 단어가 합쳐진 비속어이다. 이 표현은 창녀촌에서의 지불에 대한 가치를 얻어내고 싶은 상황에서 유래한 것 같다.

Literally "to take out or extract the pussy." *Bbong* (뽕) comes from the low expression for the female genitalia and *bbaeda* (빼다) means to take out. This may come from the concept of getting value from the fee paid for a prostitute.

물에 들어간 물고기

HaPum   피곤해. 물 나이트 별로야. 집에나 가자.

SaengTae   뭐?! 우리 방금 왔잖아.

MyongTae   안주도 방금 나왔는데. 술 마시자. 뽕빼고 놀아야지.

HaPum   뽕빼고 싶은거였으면, 우리는 왜 데리고 온거야?

HanSum   그냥 창녀촌에나 가라! 언제나 물 좋은.

Fish in the Water

하품   I'm tired. Mool isn't that fun. Let's go home.

생태   What?! We just got here.

명태   And the anju just came. Have a drink.
       Bbongbbaeda and party.

하품   Well, If you want bbongbbaeda, why did you bring us here?

한숨   Yeah, just go to the red light district!
       Where the mool is always good.

The Straight Scoop

안주 [an-ju] a Korean side dish. Many Koreans like to order *anju* when they drink alcohol at bars and nightclubs. In fact, it's expected that you order *anju* when you go to most pubs. Dishes include: dried squid or *nogari* (young pollok – think dried minnows), various nuts, tofu with *kimchi*, *pajeon* (Korean pancakes), fried chicken, or even *beondaegi*, which are roasted silkworm larvae. Yum!

삐끼

[bbi-kki]

a picker; a waiter (who grabs customers off the street)

끄는것을 의미하는 일본어 히끼로부터 변형된 비속어. 한국에서 이는 사람들(특히 여성)을 나이트에 오도록 유혹하는 점원을 묘사하는 표현이 되었다.

From the Japanese *Hikki*, meaning to pull or drag, in Korea it describes waiters who attempt to drag people (particularly women) into a nightclub by persistent or brazen means.

물 속으로 돌아가다

MyongTae 생태야, 저거 하품이 아니야? 쟤들 30분 전에 나갔잖아.

SaengTae 뭐야, 이리로 오고있어.

〔하품을 끌고 테이블로 온 웨이터는 그녀를 자리에 앉힌다.〕

SaengTae 뭐야? 너 간줄 알았는데. 한숨이는 어딨어?

HaPum 묻지도 마라. 우리도 그러려고 했는데, 밖에 있는 삐끼들이 완전 강제로 손목 잡고 끌고왔어. 한숨이는 어디로 갔는지도 모르겠어! 빌어먹을 삐끼새끼들.

MyongTae 넌 물 속에 있어야만 해. 물 나이트가 바로 그곳이야.

Back in the Water

명태 Hey SangTae, isn't that HaPum? They left a half hour ago.

생태 Look, here she comes.

[The waiter drags HaPum to the table and sits her down.]

생태 What happened? I thought you left. And where's HanSum?

하품 Don't even ask. We tried to leave, but the bbikkis outside were too forceful. They just grabbed me by the wrist and hauled me in. Now, I can't find HanSum! Fucking bbikkis.

명태 I guess you belong in the water. Mool is the place.

139

삥뜯다

[bbing-ddeut-da]

to shake down; to fleece someone

갈취를 의미. 돈을 저속히 이르는 단어, 삥과 돈을 뜯어낸다는 의미를 가지는 뜯다가 결합된 표현. 이는 어린 학생들의 돈을 갈취하는 청소년의 행위를 이르는 말로 종종 사용되며, 가끔은 남편의 돈을 뜯어내는 것에도 쓰인다.

Literally "a shake down." This expression is often used for school bullies and stems from the low expression for money, *bbing* (삥), and *ddeutda* (뜯다), meaning to extort or squeeze someone. When not used for students bullying, it refers to a wife who plucks her husband of his money.

가면 벗은 아줌마

Ajumma2	무슨 일 있어? 표정이 안좋아!
Ajumma1	남편이 날 속였어.
Ajumma2	그럼, 남편 삥뜯자. 뭘 해야할지 알고있어.
Ajumma1	정말? 난 너가 무지 순진한줄 알았는데.
Ajumma2	나 엄청 힘들고 어렵게 자랐잖아. 그래서 학교다닐 때 삥뜯는걸 배웠어. 좋아, 여기 좋은 방법이 있어…

Ajumma Unmasked

아줌마2	What's wrong? You look upset!
아줌마1	My husband is cheating on me.
아줌마2	Well, then let's bbingdeutda him. I know just what to do.
아줌마1	Really, I thought you were so innocent.
아줌마2	I grew up poor and tough, so I learned how to bbingdeutda the other girls in my class. OK, here's how we'll do it…

Slick, Scaly and Separate of Lip

Slick like a snaky swish,

separate of lip, but scaly like fish,

shiut ~ sliding through clenched teeth

touching and terrible from somewhere beneath.

From sss to shhhh

Starting soft and seething, then rising to a shoosh.

It's there for a sec, then gone in a whoosh.

사오정

[sa-o-jeoung]

a moron; an idiot or an imbecile

사오정은 중국전설에 등장하는 인물로, 한국만화에서는 귀가 거의 안들려서 멍청한 행동을 하는 캐릭터로 그려졌다. 이 표현은 누군가 질문을 잘못 알아듣고, 엉뚱한 대답을 할 때 종종 쓰인다.

Saojeoung is a legendary Chinese person who has become a character in a Korean animated series. He is portrayed as an thickheaded fool since he is almost completely hearing impaired. He is often unaware of what is going on, and misunderstands those around him. The phrase is often used for someone who answers a different question than was asked, or just doesn't get the joke.

Synonym: 형광등 [hyeong-gwang-deung] a dim, flickering light (read: dimwit).

지독한 귀머거리 배트맨

Robin	야, 배트맨. 악당들이 여기 쳐들어왔어!
Batman	물론이지, 여기 동굴이야. 우린 여기 있고.
Robin	아니, 악당들이 여기 왔다고! 우리가 가서 한방 먹여줄까?
Batman	악당들? 우리가 걔네들을 왜 먹여줘?
Robin	배트맨!
Batman	팻맨이라고 그만 좀 불러! 나 그렇게 뚱뚱하지 않아!
Robin	배트맨! 이 빌어먹을 사오정. 나 혼자 한방 먹이러 간다.
Batman	나도 초콜렛 갖다줘. 혼자 다 먹지말고.

Holy Bad Ears Batman

로빈	Hey Batman, the bad guys are here!
배트맨	Of course, the 'bat cave' is here. We're in it!
로빈	No, the *bad guys* are here! We've got to beat them.
배트맨	Bad guys?! Why would we 'feed them'?
로빈	Batman!
배트맨	And stop calling me a 'fat man'! I'm not that fat!
로빈	Batman! You're a fucking saojeoung. I'll fight them myself.
배트맨	Get me some chocolate too! Don't bite them all yourself!

삽질하다

[sab-jil-ha-da]

to do something pointless; a wasted effort

도랑을 파는 것. 한국에서의 군복무는 필수적이며, 복무기간 중 이유없이 땅을 파야하는 경우가 종종 있다. 이 때문에 무의미한 일을 일컫는 표현이 되었다. 이와 비슷한 영어표현 으로는 "헛다리 짚다"가 있다.

Literally "to dig a ditch." Korean military service is mandatory, and there is often nothing for the conscripts to do but dig ditches – hence to do useless work. Distantly related to the English expression "shoveling shit," or even "barking up the wrong tree," but also related to BS or bullshitting someone.

휴가 중

〔병식의 폰이 울린다〕

HwaSeok	야, 민희 전화야? 아름이에 대해서 좀 물어봐. 나 좋아한대?
ByungShik	아니. 창현이랑 삽질에 대한 얘기야.
HwaSeok	우린 휴가 중이잖아. 또 땅 파래? 대장 농땡이 때문에? 그 개새끼가 우리 오래?
ByungShik	아니, 멍청아. 아름이는 너 안 좋아해. 민희가 너한테 삽질하지 말라고 말해달라는거야. 아름이는 지금 창현이랑 사귀고 있다고.

On Leave

[ByungShik's phone rings]

화석	Hey, is that MinHee? Ask her about Arum. Does she like me?
병식	Nope. It's about ChangHyun and sabjilhada.
화석	But we're on leave. We have to dig ditches again? Cause of Corporal Nongddaengi? Is that SOB calling us in?
병식	No, you dope. Arum doesn't like you, so MinHee told me to tell you not to sabjilhada. Arum's dating ChangHyun now.

새대가리

[sae-dae-ga-ri]

to be totally oblivious; a birdbrain; a twit

새의 머리라는 뜻. 창피를 주기 위해 친구들 사이에서 쓰인다. 이것은 누군가가 바보같이 굴 때, 혹은 잘 잊어버릴 때 사용되며 이와 비슷한 영어표현으로는 "새 뇌"가 있다.

Literally "a bird's head." *Saedaegari* can be used as an insult among friends. It alludes to someone being annoyingly stupid or forgetful and is similar to calling someone a "moron," a "buffoon" or "bird brained" in English.

Also: 닭대가리 [dalk-dae-ga-ri] chicken head; 돌대가리 [dol-dae-ga-ri] rock head.

유유상종

SoYoon	지윤이 어디갔어?
HeeYeon	걔 또 까먹었나봐. 전화해보자. 완전 새대가리같애.
SoYoon	뭐? 걔 머리 작지않아. 생각해봐! 크고 각졌잖아. 깍두기처럼.
HeeYeon	아니, 내 말은 새대가리라고. 새 뇌 같이 잘 까먹고. 전화해봐!
SoYoon	야 새대가리… 어디야? 집이야? 튀어나와!

Birds of a Feather

소윤	Where's JiYoon?
회연	I bet she forgot again. Let's call her. She's such a saedaegari.
소윤	What? She doesn't have a small head. Look at it! Its big and square, like a ggakdugi.
회연	No I mean saedaegari. Forgetful, like a bird brain. Call, her!
소윤	Hey saedaegari…. Where are you? At home? Get out here!

The Straight Scoop

깍두기 [ggak-du-gi] - a type of kimchi made from Chinese radish usually cut into small bite-sized cubes.

시원하다

[si-won-ha-da]

to hit the spot; what a relief; whew!

글자 그대로는 선선하고 서늘하다라는 뜻 (추운것과 같이). 비속어로 쓰일 때 이는 개운한 감정을 의미한다. 이는 친구들 사이에서 장난스럽게, 특히 화장실 다녀온 후 자주 사용한다.

Literally "it's cool" (as in a bit brisk or bracing). Here it refers to the cool sensation of feeling refreshed or revitalized after "relieving" oneself in the bathroom. Used jokingly among friends, particularly males, it is most often used to describe the relaxing feeling of voiding one's bladder.

따뜻한 물

WonDong   수영 어땠어?

TaeYong   와우, 정말 시원했어.

WonDong   시원했다고? 말도안돼! 너 진짜 안에서 싼거야? 미친새끼야!
나 바로 옆 레인에 있었다고!

TaeYong   나를 위한 시원함. 그리고 너를 위한 따뜻함. ㅋㅋ

Warm Water

원동   How was your swim?

태용   Wow, that was siwonhada.

원동   Siwonhada?! You didn't! Did you really go in the pool?
You ass! I was in the next lane!

태용   Siwonhada for me and warm for you. Kh kh.

새되다

[sae-doe-da]

to be made a fool of; put in an awkward position

글자 그대로, 새가 되다. 일어나지않을 일을 기대하고 기다리는등의 어리석은 행동을 한 것. 이와 관련있는 영어표현은 다음과 같다. "여기 황무지에서 우리는 새처럼 앉아있다…"

Literally "to become a bird." This relates to feeling foolish when doing something absurd or awkward like waiting for someone who is not coming or something that is just not going to happen. This vaguely correlates to the English expression: "Here we sit like birds in the wilderness…"

정신나간 새

ByungShik   너 아름이한테 또 전화하는거야? 너 그러다가 새된다.

HwaSeok   나 이미 새됐어. 이번 전화 안받으면, 황무지의 새처럼 여기서 영원히 앉아 기다릴거야.

ByungShik   뭐? 그냥 아름이는 잊어버리고 떠나.

HwaSeok   절대. 창현이가 말한 것 처럼. "나는 야생동물이 스스로 불쌍하다고 여기는건 본 적 없다. 새는 나무에서 떨어져 얼어죽을 때도 스스로 불쌍하다 여기지 않지." 아름이도 야생이고, 아름이는 꼭 올거야.

ByungShik   넌 그냥 새가 아니야, 정신나간 새지.

Loony Bird

병식   Are you calling Arum again? You're saedoeda.

화석   I'm already saedoeda. Now if she doesn't answer, I'll sit here forever like a bird in the wilderness.

병식   What? Forget about her and move on.

화석   Never. Like ChangHyun told us. "I never saw a wild thing sorry for itself. A bird will fall frozen dead from a bough without ever having felt sorry for itself." She's a wild thing too, and she'll come.

병식   You're not just a bird, you're a loony bird.

Korean Superstitions

Myth, Legend and Delusionary Illusions

- 비오는 날에는 회를 먹지마라.

  [bi-o-neun nal-oe-neun hui-reul meok-ji-ma-ra]

  If you eat sushi on a rainy day, you will get a stomachache.

- 시험보기 전 날 미역국 먹으면 시험에서 떨어진다. [si-heom-bo-gi jeon nal mi-yeok-gug meok-eu-myeon si-heom-oe-seo ddeor-eo-jin-da]

  If you eat *miyokguk* the day before a test, you will fail – it is slippery soup, and so you will slip and fall. (Korean slang for failing a test is to fall off.)

- 시험보기 전 날 엿을 먹으면 시험에 붙는다.

  [si-heom-bo-gi jeon nal yeot-eul meok-eu-myeon si-heom-ae but-neun-da]

  If you eat yot (엿) the day before a test, you will succeed – it is sticky, and so you will pass... because you won't slip and fall.

- 동짓날에는 팥죽을 먹어야한다.

  [dong-jit-nal-oe-neun pat-juk-eul meok-eo-ya-han-da]

  You should eat red bean soup on the Winter Solstice (Traditionally, Koreans thought that sprinkling red bean soup on the ground will ward off goblins), and for some, dog soup or young chicken with ginseng soup on the Summer Solstice (purely for good health, of course).

- 감옥에서 나오면 두부를 먹어야한다.

  [gam-ok-oe-seo na-o-myeon du-bu-reul meok-eo-ya-han-da]

  When you get out of prison, you need to have a tofu party.
  (The white tofu signifies purity)

- 빨간 글씨로 이름을 쓰면 죽는다.

  [bbal-gan geul-ssi-ro i-rum-eul sseu-myeon juk-neun-da]

  Write your name in red, and you will die. (In Korean ancestral rites, the name of the dead person is written on a piece of paper in red.)

- 돼지 꿈을 꾸면 돈이 들어온다.

  [due-ji ggum-eul ggu-myeon don-i deur-eo-on-da]

  If you dream about a pig, you will have luck with money.

- 도둑질하고 그 집에 똥싸면 안 들킨다.

  [do-dok-jil-ha-go geu jib-ae ddong-ssa-myeon an deul-kin-da]

  If a thief poops at the house he steals from, he cannot be caught.

섹끈하다

[soek-ggeun-ha-da]

foxy and fabulous; tight; shit hot; slammin'

글자 그대로 해석하면, 끈끈한 섹시. 섹시함을 뜻하는 섹이라는 첫 글자와 끈끈함으로부터 온 끈이라는 글자가 합쳐져 대단히 좋음, 훌륭함을 의미하게 되었다. 보통 자동차 등 멋진 물건을 표현할 때 쓰이지만 여성에게 쓰이면 부정적인 의미를 가질 수도 있다.

Literally "to be tenaciously sexy." Beginning with *soek* (섹) for sexy and ending with *ggeun* (끈) for tenacity, this expression is used to describe someone or something as cool or fabulous. Usually used for a car or other item, but when referring to a woman it would have the connotation of "slutty." Also spelled *sae-ggeun-ha-ta* (새끈하다).

완전 죽인다!

Peter	한국어로 'cool'은 어떻게 얘기해?
Changhyun	음, '대단하다.'
Peter	아니, 아니. 그건 너무 식상해. 그것보다 더 재밌는 표현들 많잖아… 영어로 한다면, fresh, phat, off the hook, the bomb, slammin,' hot, badass, the shit, 뭐 이런거.
Changhyun	많지. 어… 좋다, 멋있다, 간지난다, 죽인다…
Peter	아니 그것도 말고, 내가 뭔가를 멋지고 아름답고 섹시하다고 한번에 말하고 싶을 때는 뭐라고하면 되냐고.
Changhyun	아, 그건 쉽지. 그냥 섹끈하다고 말해.

So cool!

피터	How do you say 'cool' in Korean?
창현	Um, 'taedanhada.'
피터	No, no. That's too dull. It's got to be more interesting than that… In English, there's fresh, phat, off the hook, the bomb, slammin', hot, badass, the shit, etc.
창현	There's so many. Uh… 'chota, moshita, ganjinanda, chuginda…'
피터	No, I want to say that something's cool and beautiful and sexy all at the same time.
창현	Oh, that's easy? Just say it's soekggeunhada.

A Look at 'Looks'

♂ To a guy

Handsome (멋있다)

- 미남 [mi-nam] beautiful man
- 훈남 [hun-nam] heartwarming man
- 완소남 [wueon-so-nam] perfectly precious man
- 꽃미남 [ggot-mi-nam] flower beautiful man
- 킹카 [king-ka] king hot in a group/school/class

Ugly (추한)

- 추남 [chu-nam] homely guy

♀ To a girl

Pretty (예쁘다)

- 미녀 [mi-nyeo] beautiful woman
- 훈녀 [hun-nyeo] heart-warming woman
- 완소녀 [wueon-so-nyeo] perfectly precious woman
- 꽃미녀 [ggot-mi-nyeo] flower-beautiful woman
- 퀸카 [kueen-ka] queen hot in one's group, school or class
- 베이글녀 [bae-i-geul-nyeo] bagel girl – a glamorous, baby-faced girl

Ugly (소박해 보이는)

- 추녀 [chu-nyeo] homely girl

⚥ To either

Good looking (잘 생긴)

- 섹시 [saek-si] sexy
- 섹끈 [saek-ggeun] cool
- 몸짱 [moem-jjang] rockin' body
- 얼짱 [eol-jjang] flawless face
- 죽인다 [juk-in-da] to die for
- 착하다 [chak-ha-da] in great shape
- 볼매 [bol-mae] get better over time, grow on someone

Ugly (추한못 생긴)

- 못난이 [mot-nan-i] just didn't come out well
- 얼꽝 [eol-ggwang] a 'nada' face
- 폭탄 [pok-tan] a bomb or a grenade – not to be confused with the American "the bomb," which means the opposite and closer to the expression "Falling on a grenade."

식후땡

[shik-hu-ddaeng]

after dinner smoke; post-meal blaze

간단히, '먹는 것'을 뜻하는 한자 '식', '이후'를 뜻하는 한자 '후' 그리고 지포라이터를 열 때 나는 '땡그랑 소리'를 의미하는 의성어 '땡'이 결합된 비속어이다.

So simple: *shik* (식) is the Chinese character for "eating," *hu* (후) is the Chinese character for "after" and *ddaeng* (땡) is onomatopoeia for "with a clang," as in the clang of a Zippo lighter being opened.

Also: 식곤증 [shik-ku-jeung] after dinner drowsiness

담배 피워줘서 고마워 2

Siwoo	밖에 잠깐 나갔다 올께.
Peter	뭐? 식후땡하러? 너 담배 끊은거 아니였어?
Siwoo	음, 글쎄...
Peter	우리 얘기하고 있었잖아. 치, 매너없어!
Siwoo	아니야, 이게 매너 좋은거지. 어른 앞에서 담배 피우면 안되잖아!
Peter	그럼 내가 고맙다고 해야되나?

Thank You for Smoking 2

시우	I'm going outside.
피터	What? For a shikhuddaeng? Didn't you quit smoking?
시우	Uh, well...
피터	We're in the middle of a conversation. Ts, no manners!
시우	No, its good manners. I can't smoke in front of my elders!
피터	So should I say thanks?

Culturally Speaking

Well...

글쎄... [geul-ssae] Koreans tend to avoid confrontation, so rather than saying 'yes' and risk being caught in a lie, or 'no' and flat out lying, one might say "well..." or simply not answer and look down in a show of repentance.

150

싸가지없다

[ssa-ga-ji-eob-da]

an ill-mannered sod; a douche; a jerk

글자 그대로, 운이 없다. 좋은 징조, 행운을 뜻하는 싹수라는 단어에서 변형된 싸가지와 존재하지 않음을 뜻하는 없다라는 단어가 합쳐진 표현이다. 이 비속어는 매너없는 이는 곧 행운도 없음을 반영하고 있다. 새끼와 함께 종종 사용된다.

Literally meaning "no luck." *Ssagaji* (싸가지) comes from *ssaksu* (싹수) meaning "a good omen" or "luck" and *eobda* (없다) simply means "there is none." In a sense, it suggests that one without manners will have no luck and therefore no basis for a future. It is often used before a swear word such as SOB and has the connotation of a jerk, an ass or a douchebag.

Synonyms: 재수없다 [jae-su-eob-da] karma's a bitch (it will get you); 버릇없다 [beo-reut-eob-da] impudent fool; 싹수가 없다 [ssak- eob-da] a certain failure

까치에게 온 좋지 않은 징조

Ggachi	어떡하지, 내가 교수 빡돌게 한 것 같아.
Jaebi	무슨 일 있었어?
Ggachi	내가 교수한테 말대꾸했더니 난 시험 볼 운도 없을거랬어.
Jaebi	싸가지없는 새끼.
Ggachi	그래. 교수는 싸가지없는 놈일 수 있겠지만,
	난 여전히 운이 없네.

A Bad Omen for the Magpie

까치	Oh man, I think I pissed off my professor.
제비	How did you do that?
까치	I disagreed with him and he said I'd have no luck on the exam.
제비	That ssagajieobneun SOB.
까치	Yeah, he may be a ssagajieobda bastard, but I'm still out of luck.

이 부장

쌍수

[ssang-su]

double-eyelid surgery; creating the crease; an eye job

쌍꺼풀 수술의 줄임말. 쌍꺼풀 수술은 이렇듯 약어로까지 쓰이는, 매우 흔한 성형수술이다.

An abbreviation of *ssang-keo-pul su-sul* (쌍커풀 수술), or double-eyelid surgery. A procedure to reproduce the fold in eyelids common to Westerners, this type of cosmetic surgery is so widespread that its short form is in common use.

강남역 스타일

Param	와, 저 여자 옆모습 좀 봐. 홀딱 반했어! 분명히 TenPro일거야!
SunSu	뭐?! 너가 정면에서 못 봐서 그래.
Param	그게 무슨 소리야?.
SunSu	쌍수가 되다 말았어. 얼굴이 완전 이상해.
Param	괜찮아. 난 독창적인 것을 좋아하니까. 다 똑같은 얼굴은 싫다고.
SunSu	한 대 맞은 얼굴 같다니까!
Param	강남역 스타일은 잊어버려, 저게 바로 내 스타일이야.

Gangnam Station Style

바람	Wow, look at her profile. I'm smitten! She must be a TenPro!
선수	What?! You obviously haven't seen her from the front.
바람	Why do you say that?
선수	Her ssangsu didn't take. She's totally lopsided.
바람	It's all right. I dig originality. I don't want a clone.
선수	She looks like she had a stroke!
바람	Forget Gangnam Station Style, that's MY style.

The Straight Scoop

강남역 스타일 (Gangnam Station Style) there are so many cosmetic surgery hospitals turning out "beauty" clones near Gangnam station that Gangnam Station Style refers to the plastic girls that all try to look the same. And far too much surgery would produce a 성괴 (*song-goe*) or plastic monster.

싸이숨 (P'sigh)

[ssa-i-sum]

a Psy lament; sick of seeing Psy

싸이를 보는 것에 대한 넌더리. 또 다른 비디오, TV 광고, 인터뷰 등에서 싸이를 보는 것에 대한 무의식적인 반응이다. "아 저기 싸이 또 나와, 그래… 그러던지 말던지. 난 정말 강남 스타일에 질렸어!"

An unconscious reaction to seeing Psy in yet another video, TV commercial, on a show, being interviewed, etc. "Oh, there's Psy again, yeah… whatever. I'm so over Gangnam Style!"

내쉬다

HanSum	아, 싸이숨…
HaPum	헐. 무슨 말이야?!
HanSum	싸이 춤이 나오는, 벌써 세 번째 똑 같은 광고야. 누가 날 좀 죽여줘요!
HaPum	어, 나도 그래. 저 노래, 저 춤, 그리고 저 포동포동한 얼굴 정말 지겨워!!
HanSum	한숨 그리고 슈퍼 싸이숨…

Exhale

한숨	Uh, P'sigh…
하품	Huhhh. What do you mean?!
한숨	That's the third commercial in a row with Psy dancing. Somebody, please kill me!
하품	Ugh, I know. I'm so sick of that song, that dance, that chubby face!!
한숨	Sigh and super P'sigh…

The Straight Scoop

텐프로 (TenPro) A girl that is pretty, educated and talented that works in the top ten percent of room salons; a top 10% prostitute.

쌩까다

[s s a e n g - g g a - d a]

to feign ignorance; pretend not to understand

문자 그대로, 쌩 – 바람처럼 윙윙소리를 내고, 휙, 휑 가는 것처럼 그냥 지나가는 것 혹은 까먹다와 같이 그저 무언가를 잊어버린 것을 의미. 이 표현은 다툰 후 누군가를 무시할 때, 혹은 주의를 기울이지 않을 때 사용된다.

Ssang (쌩) is to whistle, zip, or zing, and *ggada* could be go (가다) as in to go by or whistle by, or as with the phonetic 'peel-and-eat' of *ggamoekda* (까먹다), to just forget it. This expression can be used for ignoring someone after an argument, pretending not to understand someone's directions that you don't want to follow, or when someone is just not paying attention.

여름 캠프에서

Victor	한국 아이들은 영어를 못알아들어.
Peter	아닌데, 알아들어! 왜, 무슨 일 있어?
Victor	오두막 좀 치우라고 얘기하면 그냥 탁구나 치러 가고.
	너 한국말 할 줄 아니까 네가 얘기 좀 해봐.
Peter	오, 걔네 그냥 쌩까는거야. 이거 봐!
	창현, 쌩까지말고 지금 당장 오두막 치워!
ChangHyun	어, 알아, 알겠다고…

At Summer Camp

빅터	The Korean kids don't understand English.
피터	Yes they do! Why, what happened?
빅터	When I tell them to clean up the cabin, they just go play Ping-Pong. You speak Korean, can you tell them.
피터	Oh, they're just doing ssaengggada. Watch this! "ChangHyun, don't ssaengggada and clean the cabin now!"
창현	Yeah, I know, I know…

쌩얼

[ssaeng-eol]

au naturel; a fresh face

글자 그대로, 생의 얼굴. 신선함 혹은 날것을 의미하는 쌩과 얼굴을 의미하는 얼의 합성어이다. 전통적으로 한국인들은 집을 나오기 전에 화장하는 것을 기본적 예의로 믿었다. 하지만 요즘은 쌩얼 화장법이 유행이다.

Literally "a raw face." This is a combination of *ssaeng* (쌩) for fresh or raw and *eol* (얼) for *eolgul* (얼굴), which simply means face. Traditionally, Koreans believe that it is basic manners to apply makeup before leaving the house, but a recent trend calls for *ssaengeol*, a bare minimum of makeup or makeup that looks more natural.

독신으로 남기

JiYoon 그 얼굴 꼬라지는 뭐야? 너 선보러 나오는데 쌩얼로 온거야?
이제 너 엄마한테 죽었다!

SoYoon 아니야, 했어. 이게 바로 꾸미지 않은, 깨끗한 – 새로운 쌩얼
스타일이야. 남자들은 더이상 떡칠한 얼굴을 원하지 않는다고.

JiYoon 그래, 아무리 그래도 너 옷은 좀 갖춰 입어야하는거 아니냐?

SoYoon 뭐? 이 청바지 300,000원짜리야!

Staying Single

지윤 What kind of face is that? Did you come out with ssaengeol…
to a seon?! Mom's gonna kill you!

소윤 No, I did it. This is the new style, fresh and clean –
ssaengeol style. Guys don't want to see a girl all
covered up any more.

지윤 Yeah, but you should at least have dressed up a little?

소윤 What? These jeans were 300,000 won!

The Straight Scoop

선 [seon] a marriage introduction, usually arranged by parents of upper middle class families as a possible stepping stone to marriage.

썰렁하다

[sseol-leong-ha-da]

that's so lame; NOT funny

글자 그대로 풀이하면, 으슬으슬하고 추운 것을 뜻한다. 전통적으로 한국인들은 편안하고 재미있는 주제로 얘기하고 있는 분위기를 따뜻하고 화목함을 뜻하는 사자성어, 화기애애로 표현해왔다. 이것은 그 반대, 불편하고 재미없는 상황에서 쓰인다(또한, 한국인들이 이 표현을 사용할 때에는 마치 차가운 바람이 부는 양, 그들의 팔을 문지르곤 한다).

Literally "it's cold or chilly." Traditionally, Koreans would use the old Chinese expression *hwagiaeae* (화기애애), meaning warm and harmonious, for topics that are comfortable and fun to discuss. Its opposite, then would be something uncomfortable or chilly. (Also, when Koreans use this expression, they often rub their arms as if experiencing a sudden gust of cold wind.)

독도 여행

HaPum	(벌벌 떨며) 이 춥고 조그만 바위덩어리에 무슨 야단법석들이래용?!
HanSum	아니지... 이건 한국의 영토권에 대한 아주 중요한 이슈라고!
HaPum	그리고 놀러오기에도 참 좋네... 넌 여기 살아야 겠다.
HanSum	썰렁하다! 완전 썰렁해!
HaPum	그럼 니 쟈켓 입어용, 멍청아!
HanSum	아니! 내 말은 농담... 썰렁하다고!

Trip to Dokdo

하품	(Shivering) Is this what all the fuss is about? This cold little rock?!
한숨	No... it's a really important issue about sovereign Korean territory!
하품	And such a great place to visit... I think you should live here.
한숨	Sseolleonghada! Completely Sseolleonghae!
하품	So put your jacket on, dummy!
한숨	No! I mean the joke... it's sseolleonghada!

Culturally Speaking

Some Slick Endings for ~Post Appending

Beginnings & Endings – fun prefixes & suffixes and their usage.

~용, ~윰, 하삼, ~하셈, ~하센, ~하염, ~해염, ~하연 – all are potential endings to add flavor to any Korean sentence:

- **모하삼?** [mo-ha-sam] from **뭐하세요?**

  changes the feeling from a simple "What are you doing?" to "What's up?" or more appropriately, "Sup?"

- **어디샘?** [eo-di-saem] - from **어디세요?**

  changes the feeling from "Where are you?" to "Where you at?"

- **술마셔용** [sul-ma-sheo-yong] - from **술마셔요.**

  changes the meaning from "I'm drinking." to the deliberately cutesy "I'm drinking-ing-ing."

- **잘했쪄욤** [jal-haess-jjyeo-yeom] - from **잘했어요.**

  changes the feeling from "Good Job" to something cutesy (imagine them giving a pouty look with their lip protruding).

Ha! – There are no prefixes in Korean!! *Maerrong*! (매렁)

썸(타다)

[sseom(ta-da)]

be something to me; have chemistry or be into someone

영어 단어 "something" 의 콩글리시화 된 표현인 "썸씽"으로 사용되다가 "썸"으로 축약된 말로, 누군가가 다른 사람에게 어느 정도 관심을 갖는 것 또는 그 반대의 경우를 나타낸다. "타다"와 함께 쓰여 두 사람이 반하거나, 매력을 느끼고, 또는 어떤 화학 작용을 일으키는 "썸"의 상태가 됨을 나타낸다. "그 사람은 내 썸남/썸녀야" 와 같이 종종 남자(-남)나 여자(-녀)를 의미하는 어미와 함께 쓰인다.

Taken from the English word "something," which had been used in a Konglicized *sseomssing* (썸씽) and shortened to just *sseom* to represent someone that has some interest in someone else and vice versa. With *tada*, it becomes the status of 'some' as it to crush on, have a strong attraction or some chemistry between people. It is often used with a male (*nam*) or female (*nyeo*) ending (썸남, 썸녀) as in he's/she's something to me or could become someone special in my life.

막장 드라마

Ajumma1 〈썸남 썸녀〉라는 새로 나온 막장 드라마 봤어?

Ajumma2 뭐? 어머머머! 재밌겠다! 내용이 뭐야?

Ajumma1 음, 재벌 아들이 한 명 있는데 되게 많은 여자의 썸남이야. 그래서 어떤 평범한 여자애랑 썸을 타는데 그의 강압적인 엄마는 아들이 정치인의 딸과 결혼하기를 원하지. 그런데 그 정치인의 딸은 사실 재벌 아들의 아빠가 그 여자 엄마랑 몰래 바람을 펴서 낳은 이복동생이야. (그리고 그 두 사람은 아직도 썸을 타고 있지.) 그리고 재벌 아들 엄마랑 정치인 딸 엄마는 절친이고.

Ajumma2 확실히 짚고 넘어가자. 그는 그 여자를 좋아하고 그 여자도 그를 좋아하는데 그는 여동생과 결혼할 운명이고, 그 여동생은 사실 다른 사람에게 관심이 있고, 그의 아빠는 사실 그녀의 엄마와 썸을 타고 있지. 맞지?

Ajumma1 내말이...

Ajumma2 우와 그거 완전 썸드라마인데! ㅋㅋ

Makjang Drama

아줌마1   Have you watched the new makjang drama? It's called Sseomnam Sseomnyo.

아줌마2   What?! Oh mo-mo-mo! That sounds delicious! What's the story?

아줌마1   Well, there's this Chebol son, who's sseomnam to so many. So he's sseom to this common girl, but his overbearing mother wants him to marry a politician's daughter, but she's actually his biological half-sister from the secret affair of his father with her mother (who still have sseomtada), and her mother and his mother are best friends.

아줌마2   So let me get this straight? He's with her, and she's with him, but he's doomed to wed his sister, who's actually interested someone else, and his dad is sseom to her mom. Right?!

아줌마1   Exactly...

아줌마2   Wow, that's sseom drama! Kh, kh.

The Straight Scoop

막장 드라마 [mak-jang drama] silly Korean dramas with ridiculous premises or absurd situations.

재벌 [chae-bol] large conglomerates in Korea that are family controlled, extremely hierarchical and often have government ties. A son of such a *chaebol* would be considered a good catch by almost any Korean woman, and is about as likely as prince charming showing up on a white steed.

The Yin and Yang of Iung's Lyric

Oh what a lovely opening spread:

　　　the mouth wide; its sound unsaid,

to welcome the vowels soon to flow

　　　or round out the end with "ng" below.

　　　From ng ng ng 잉잉잉 or begun as naught

was the yin and yang of i-ung ㅇ wrought.

아다

[a-da]

a virgin

새로움, 신선함 혹은 현대적인 것을 뜻하는 일본말 아따라시로부터 유래하였다. 한국인들은 숫총각(처녀)을 의미하는 비속어로 이 단어의 일부분을 빌려왔다.

From the Japanese *atarashi*, meaning new, fresh or modern. The Koreans borrowed part of this word to use as slang for a virgin, especially for teasing someone about their lack of experience (most often a man).

아다로부터의 탈출

SiWoo 아따라시, 아따라시, 아따라시.

TaeYong 뭐하는 거야? 창현이 얘기하는거야?

SiWoo 아니, 일본어 연습하고 있는거야.

TaeYong 걔 이젠, 신선한 아다 아닌거 알아? 어제 탈출했어.

SiWoo 아, 진짜? 알았어, 아다 아니야, 아다 아니야, 아다 아니야…

Escape from Ada

시우 Atarashi, atarashi, atarashi.

태용 What are you doing? Talking about Changhyun?

시우 No, I'm practicing my Japanese.

태용 You know he's not a fresh ada anymore.

He escaped last night.

시우 Oh, really? OK, ada no more, ada no more, ada no more…

안물

[an-mul]

so what?; whatever; who cares?

예의를 차려야 하는 상황에서는 쓰일 수 없다. 안물은 한국어 '안물어봤어'의 줄임말이다. 이 표현은 빈정대는 어조로서, "야, 그만해! 누가 물어봤어?" 혹은 "아무도 신경 안 쓰거든!"의 뜻을 함축하고 있다. 이는 주로 누군가 자랑하고 있을 때 쓰이는 표현이다.

Not to be used in polite situations, *anmul* is a simple abbreviation of the Korean 안물어봤어 (an-mul-eo-buass-eo), meaning "I didn't ask you." This expression includes a note of sarcasm and carries with it the connotation of "Bitch, please! Who asked you?" or "Nobody cares!" It is most often used in response to someone who is boasting or bragging.

차례

〔그녀 아버지의 묘지에서〕

GeunHye 아버지, 어떻게 지내셨어요?
아주 훌륭한 일들을 하느라고 너무 바빴어요!

ChungHee ...

GeunHye 그리고 아버지, 아주 놀라운 소식 있어요.
저 출마해서 한국의 첫 여성 대통령으로 당선되었어요!

ChungHee ...

GeunHye 아아아아, 만약 여기 계셨더라면 정말 저를 자랑스러워 하셨을 텐데!
제가 예절의 기준 또한 다시 정립해서, fashion police들은 대거
총력을 기울이게 될 것이고...

〔무덤으로부터 구슬픈 소리가 흘러나온다〕

ChungHee 아아아아아아아안-무우우우우우울!

Charae

[at the grave site of her father]

근해   Daddy, how have you been? I've been so busy doing great things!

정희   …

근해   And Daddy, I have amazing news. I ran for office and
I just became the first female president of Korea!

정희   …

근해   Ahhh, if you were only here, daddy, you would be so proud of me!
I've even brought back the standards of decency,
the fashion police are in full force and…

[wailing comes from the grave]

정희   Aaaaaannn-muuuuuulllll!

The Straight Scoop

차례 [cha-rae] - the act of praying at one's ancestor's gravesite. This practice is often observed on the traditional Korean holidays of Solnal (Lunar New Year's) and Chuseok (Thanksgiving Day)

왜 씹어?

[wae sshib-eo]

why don't you answer?; why you ducking me?

문자 그대로는 "왜 너 나를 씹고(음식을 씹듯) 있어?" 라는 의미. 이 표현은 잡담하는 것 이외에 정말 할 일이 없을 때 쓰인다. 사실 문자 그대로의 의미와는 정반대로 누군가의 말, 특히 문자메시지에 회신을 하지 않을 때 하는 말이다. 또한 "씹지마"라는 표현은 "내 메시지 모른 척 하지 마"라는 의미이다.

Literally "Why are you masticating me?" This expression has nothing to do with "chewing the fat." In fact, it is quite the opposite. It is about chewing someone's words, or more specifically a text message, and simply ignoring it or failing to answer in a reasonable amount of time. Similar to getting the "brush off" or being "blown off" by someone who would rather just ignore you than just come out and say something to clarify, like "Bite me! "

Also: 씹지마 [ship-ji-ma] for "stop ducking me," or literally, "Don't chew me."

27개의 문자 메시지

Arum   왜 씹어?

ChangHyun   뭐? 씹어?! 나 아무것도 씹고 있지 않아… 점심 먹을 시간 없거든.

Arum   아니, 왜 내 메시지에 회신 안 하냐고!

ChangHyun   네가 1시간 동안 메시지를 27개나 보냈잖아!

Arum   그건 그렇지만, 나 안보고 싶어?!

ChangHyun   아, 지겨워! 나 지금 일하고 있잖아! 나 좀 혼자 내버려 둬!

ChangHyun   그 년 때문에 정말 미쳐버리겠어!

SiWoo   임마, 그만 좀 씹어. 여자친구 욕을 그렇게 하면 안되지.

ChangHyun   아, 갠 도대체 어떻게 알아차린 거지?!

SiWoo   너 전화 안 끊었어! 네 여자친구 다 듣고 있어, 멍충이.

ChangHyun   오, 젠장!

27 Texts

아름	Why you shibeo?
창현	Huh? Chewing?! I'm not chewing anything... I don't have time for lunch.
아름	No, why don't you answer my messages?
창현	You've sent me 27 messages in the last hour!
아름	But, don't you miss me?!
창현	Ah, chigyeowo! (interminable!) I'm at work! Leave me alone!
창현	That bitch is driving me crazy!
시우	Dude, don't shibeo, you shouldn't talk shit about your girl.
창현	Ah, how is she going to find out?!
시우	You never hung up! She's still on the line, dumbass!
창현	Oh, shit!

씹어 [sshib-eo] to talk behind someone's back; slander or speak ill of; talk shit about someone.

안습

[an-seup]

I saw what I shouldn't see; it's so bad, I'm gonna cry

문자그대로 '안구에 습기차다'의 줄임말이다. 이것은 안구의 안과 습기차다의 습의 두 글자를 합친말로서, 나쁜 냄새 때문에 눈물이 나오는 것처럼 안 좋은 상황을 보았을 때 사용되는 비속어이다.

Literally "to tear up" or "have moist eyeballs." Here it means something so sad and pathetic that you'd rather not see or hear about. *Anseup* is an acronym stemming from the *an* (안) of *angu* (안구), meaning eyeball and the *seup* (습) of *seup-ki-cha-da* (습기차다), meaning to become moist. As in something so blindingly bad that makes your eyes water, like a bad smell or staring at the sun.

폴리에스테르 해스더

MinHee	무슨 일 있어? 울고 있는 거야?
SoYoon	어, 고등학교 천문학 시간이 떠올라서...
MinHee	오 안돼! 너 그 선생 말하는거야?
	우우. 뷁! (매스꺼움의 표현)
SoYoon	그래, 바로 그 폴리에스테르 헤스터.
MinHee	울게 생겼구만. 나도 그 큰 여자가 꽉 조이는 폴리에스테르 바지 입고있던 것 떠오를 때마다 안습.

Polyester Hester

민희	What's the matter? Are you crying?
지윤	Uhh, I just had a flashback from High School Astronomy...
민희	Oh no! You mean *the* teacher?
	Oooo. Blech! [expression of disgust]
지윤	Yeah, none other than Polyester Hester.
민희	No wonder you're crying. I get anseup every time I think of that massive woman in those over-tight polyester pants.

The Straight Scoop

뷁 [buelk] gagging sound, like *heol* indicates disinterest or disgust: meh, blech, eww.

야리다

[ya-ri-da]

to eyeball someone; squint and stare; scowl or glare at

여러분, 시우는 이 단어가 비속어로 시작된 아무런 이유도 찾지 못했습니다. 그래서 시우는 여러분의 이해를 돕기 위해 나름대로의 이야기를 만들었습니다. 옛날, 옛날에, 리씨 성을 가진 사팔뜨기 사내가 살고 있었는데, 그 사내가 사람들을 노려볼 때마다 사람들은 야! 리다. 를 외치기 시작했고 이 때문에 지금의 야리다가 되었다고 합니다. 하지만 나는 이것이 야! 왜 째리다? 의 축약형이라고 생각하는데, 과연 누가 맞는 것 같나요?

Ladies and gentlemen, Siwoo could find no origin for how this word came to be slang for staring, so he created a story behind it to help. A long, long time ago, there was a guy named Mr. Lee with a squint eye, and if he stared at people, they would say *Ya*, there's Lee – hence, *ya-Lee-(i)da* or *yarida*. Actually, I believe it's a shortened form of saying "Ya! Why are you leering at me?" (*Ya! Wae jjaerida?* or *yarida*). So who do you think is right?

저자들의 결투

Peter   야! 왜 그렇게 노려봐?

SiWoo   (대답하지 않는다. 계속 야린다)

Peter   야려보지 말라고! 니가 원하던대로 썼으니까.

Dueling Authors

피터   Ya! Why are you looking at me like that?

시우   (Doesn't answer. Continues to yarida)

피터   Don't yarida me! I wrote what you wanted…

양다리

[yang-da-ri]

to two-time someone; play the field; cheat on someone

문자 그대로 양 쪽 다리를 말하며 두 다리를 다른 두 사람의 다리 위에 걸쳐 놓는 것을 의미한다. 이것은 한 명이 동시에 두 사람과 데이트하는 것을 말한다. 이와 비슷한 영어표현으로는 "Playing the field"가 있다, 하지만 데이트와 아무 관계 없는 영어표현, "바지 입을 때에는 한 다리씩 입을 것"과 혼동하지 않도록.

Literally "both legs," suggesting that someone has each of one's legs over another person's leg at the same time. One can infer that the person is dating two (or more) people at the same time. Related to the English expression "playing the field," but not to be confused with "put on one's pants one leg at a time," which has nothing to do with dating or cheating for that matter.

이쁜 다리

Ted	즐기자, 빌. 이쁜 니 여자친구는 어딨냐?
Bill	'빌-마을' 전부 엑썰런트하지가 않구나.
Ted	무슨 일 있어? 너 미친듯 사랑에 빠진줄 알았는데?
Bill	그랬었지, 근데 걔가 양다리 걸쳤거든.
Ted	걔 다리 참 예뻤었는데… 그래서 어느쪽이 니 다리였냐? 하하
Bill	이리와. 아주 다리를 부러뜨려줄테니까!!

Good Legs

테드	Party on, Bill. Where's your beautiful girlfriend?
빌	All is not excellent in *Bill-ville*.
테드	What happened? I thought you were madly in love?
빌	I was, but she did yangdari.
테드	She had great legs though… So which leg was yours? Ha ha!
빌	Come here and I'm gonna break your legs!!

양아치

[y a n g - a - c h i]

a wannabe gangster; a hooligan

본래 뜻은 넝마주이 (그게 뭐지...? 오래된 옷이나 종이 따위를 재활용 하기 위해 모으는 사람이란다.) 비속어로 이것은, 저자 피터씨와 같이 깡패가 되고 싶은 이를 일컫는다. 보통 양아치는 약하고, 불량한 학생, 언제나 욕하며 문제를 일으킨다.

Originally a ragpicker (whatever that is…? A collector of used clothing or paper for recycling.) As slang, it refers to someone like Siwoo, a wannabe, gangster or gangbanger, or just a two-bit hood. A *yangachi* is usually overly confident and conceited, but generally weak, a bad student, always swearing and always, always in trouble.

미국산 갈비

SeungMan	질 좋은 미국산 갈비 먹으러 가자.
DaeJung	농담하냐? 너 광우병 걸리고 싶어?!
SeungMan	그건 그저 광불평일 뿐이야.
	내가 아직도 자리에 있다면, 아무도 불평 못했을텐데.
DooWhan	그래, 명박이는 너무 약해. 그 양아치는 고기도 못 먹고.
MyungBak	야, 뒷땅까지마!... 나 현대에서 일했어! 청계천도 만들었고!
	나 벼락 양아치 된 거 아니다. 난 셀러리맨의 신화라고!

American Kalbi

승만	Let's go get some good-ole American kalbi (marinated ribs).
대중	Are you kidding? Do you want to get mad cow disease?!
승만	That's just mad griping.
	If I were in power, no one would complain.
두환	Yeah, MyungBak is too weak. That yangachi can't even eat meat.
명박	Hey, stop talking shit about me!... I worked at Hyundai! I built Cheongaechon! I'm no upstart yangachi.
	I'm a MADE MAN!

엄창 (엄창)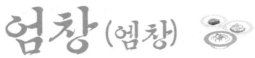

[eom-chang]

on my mother's honor; cross my heart

이것이 만약 거짓말이면, 우리 엄마는 창녀다. 엄마의 엄과 창녀의 창, 두 글자가 합쳐진 단어.(이 표현은 비교적 예전에 많이 쓰였으나, 현재도 유용하다.)

Literally "if it's a lie my mother is a harlot." Another acronym, the *eom* (엄) of *omma* (엄마) or mom, and the *chang* (창) of *changnyo* (창녀) or prostitute and is often accompanied by a gesture. (Though a bit dated, this expression is still useful.)

차 이야기

YuJa	너 둥글레네 엄마가 창녀인거 알고 있었어?
PaJeon	오미자?! 진짜로?
YuJa	정말로. 그게 바로 둥글레 이름이 긴 이유였어.
PaJeon	엄창? 못 믿겠어. 엄마 걸고 맹세해봐!
YuJa	알았어, 알았어, 엄창!

Tea Talk

유자	Did you know that DoongGeullae's mother is a harlot.
파전	OmiJa?! Are you sure?
유자	Absolutely. That's why his name is so long.
파전	Eomchang? I don't believe you. Swear on your mother!
유자	OK, OK, eomchang!

일잠

[il-jam]

turn in early

일잠은 두 개의 머리글자로 된 말로서, 일찍 잠자다에서 생겨났다. '늦게까지 잠자다'를 의미하는 늦잠이라는 반대 말로부터 생겨난 신조어이다.

Iljam is an acronym and comes from *iljjik jamjada* (일찍 잠자다), "to go to sleep early." It was coined, in response to its opposite, *neutjam* (늦잠), meaning to sleep late or sleep in.

이른 새...

Kaeul	자기야, 나 내일까지 자고싶어.
Bom	우리 일잠중이니까, 그럴 필요 없어.
Kaeul	일잠... 일잠이 뭔데?
Bom	늦잠의 반대.
Kaeul	단어 좀 그만 만들어!!

The Early Bird...

가을	Honey, I want to sleep in tomorrow...
봄	But since we are doing iljam, we don't have to.
가을	Iljam... What is iljam?
봄	The opposite of neutjam (sleeping in).
가을	Stop making up words!!

여병추

[yeo-byeong-chu]

ya bonehead; you are such a retard

'여기 병신 추가요'라는 문장으로부터, 앞의 글자들이 때어져 만들어진 비속어. 이것은 바보같은 짓을 하는 친한 친구를 놀릴 때 사용된다. 음식점에서 추가 주문을 할 때 쓰는 표현과 비슷하다.

An acronym meaning "insert retard here," *yeobyeongchu* comes from the sentence *yeo-gi* (here) *byeong-shin* (retard) *chu-ga-yo* (another please). Used when teasing a close friend for doing something stupid, it is similar to the expression used in restaurants for asking for additional orders similar to "another round please."

딤섬 레스토랑

ByungShik	중국음식 너무 좋아. 더 시키자.
KwangSung	이미 많이 먹었잖아. 그러다 배 터지겠다.
ByoungShik	그래도 더 먹고싶어! 그리고 맥주도 더!
HwaSeok	(웨이터에게 잔뜩 취해서는) 여기, 맥주 몇 병 더 추가요.
KwangSung	여병추! 너네 둘 다, 여병추!

Dim-Some Restaurant

병식	I love Chinese food. Let's order more.
광성	You've eaten so much, you look like you'll explode.
병식	But I want more! And more beer!
화석	[Drunkenly, to the waiter] Over here, more bottles of beer.
광성	Yeobyeongchu! Both of you, Yeobyeongchu!

Lost in Translation

(non)Sense and (lack of) Sensibility

OK, from dumb to crazy, the odd and the idiotic, from the inane to the insane, the brainless to the senseless, here are several slang expressions to describe your friends and enemies complete lack of sense:

- **눈치없다** [nun-chi-eob-da]

  to have no sense of a situation (particularly in social settings)

- **어리버리하다** [eo-ri-beo-ri-ha-da]

  to look disoriented, dazed and bewildered; to be dull or stupid.

- **오덕후** [o-deok-hu]

  a nerd, with an odd or unusual interest (from otaku of Japanese anime)

- **얼빵하다** [eol-bbang-ha-da]

  to look foolish, from *eolbbajida* (얼빠지다) – to be stupefied with fear, dazed, look blank, absent-minded.

- **빙시** [bing-shi], or **븅신** [byung-shin] etc.

  there are many slight sound variations for 병신 (*byungshin*) literally meaning a person with a disease or disability, but implying that someone is retarded (and including all the politically-incorrect offensiveness of the English word "retard").

- **또라이** [ddo-ra-i]

  literally, to turn or spin (of a child [ai] turning [ddol]), this slang is like the twirling of one's index finger next to one's head.

- **맛이 갔다** [mas-i gat-da]

  literally, the taste has gone [bad], and meaning for something to have gone rotten, or be off.

- **싸이코** [ssa-i-ko]

  from the English psycho [in Japanese this can mean cool too, but Koreans only use it for someone that is crazy].

- **무개념** [mu gae-nyum] **개념없다** [gae-nyum-eob-da]

  an offensive term for a total lack of common sense, like "shit for brains"

영계

[yeong-gyae]

a chick; a bird; a (yummy) hunny

글자 그대로는, 어린 닭. 이 표현은 자신보다 훨씬 어린 이성을 얘기할 때 쓰인다. 상세하게는, 이것은 남자보다는 여자에게 많이 사용되며, 일컬어지는 대상은 예쁘고, 신선하고 성적대상이 될 수 있어야 한다. 더러운 늙은 남자들은 길거리에서 젊고 예쁜 여자들에 관해 이야기하고, 아줌마들은 젊은 청년들을 향해 구구 울며…

Literally "a spring chicken," this expression is used to talk about someone much younger than oneself. In particular, it is used for young girls more than guys, and the person should be pretty, fresh and of sexual age. Dirty old men talking about some young pretty girl on the street, *ajummas* cooing over some young stud, etc.

Synonym: 로린이 [lo-lin-i] a lolita (combination of *eorini* (child) and lolita).

치킨 아니면 소고기

Flight Attendant	치킨으로 드릴까요? 아님 소고기?
Batman	영계? 자기, 이름이 뭐야?
Robin	배트맨, 여자좀 놔둬라…
	캣우먼은 어때?
Batman	아, 걔는 이제 더이상 영계가 아니잖아?
Robin	그럼 넌 늙은 수탉… 열라 늙은!
Batman	그래도 이 여자 조낸 예뻐. 알았다, 알았어, 소고기로 줘요.
Flight Attendant	죄송합니다, 고기는 다 나갔어요.

Chicken or beef

승무원	Chicken or beef.
배트맨	Spring chicken? What's your name, honey?
로빈	Batman, leave her alone… what about Catwoman?
배트맨	Ah, she's no yeonggyae anymore.
로빈	And you are an old cock… dreadfully old!
배트맨	But she's awfully cute. All right, all right, I'll have the beef.
승무원	Sorry, we're out of beef.

174

The Very 'Very' Box

Seriously... So Mega-Much

**There must be hundreds (read - *a shit ton*) of ways to say "very" in Korean...
Here are just a few.**

- 겁나게 [gop-na-gae] enough to inspire fear.
- 대따 [dae-dda] changed from *daedanhi* [대단히] meaning very, very much.
  Also: 대땅 [dae-ddang] or 대빵 [dae-bbang].
- 디따 [di-dda] a lot (or a whole helluva lot)
- 레알 [rae-al] real or really (from the English for totally).
- 매우 [mae-woo] greatly, exceedingly, remarkably.
- 무지무지 [mu-ji-mu-ji] an intensifier meaning "very, very."
  From 무지하게 [mu-ji-ha-gae]
- 아주 [a-joo] very much (simply stated).
- 엄청 [um-chung] exorbitant, preposterous, extraordinary.
- 엄청나게 [um-chung-na-gae] exorbitantly.
- 열나게 [yeol-na-gae] feverishly, vehemently, agitatedly.
  Also: 열라 [yeol-la] or 열라리 [yeol-la-li]
- 왕창 [wang-chang] from *wang* [왕] or king, as in "as much as a king's share."
- 좆나 [jot-na] literally the penis, *jot* [좆] and *naoda* [나오다], to come out. In other words, "enough to make me hard."
  Also: 좆나게 [jon-na-gae] 존나 [jon-na] 조낸 [jo-naen] or 졸라 [jol-la].
- 좆빠지게 [jot-bba-ji-gae] from *jot* (좆) for the penis and *bbajida* (빠지다) to loose or fall off. In other words, "enough to make my dick fall off."
- 지대 [ji-dae] vast, enormous. From 제대로 [jae-dae-ro] meaning totally or completely.
- 허벌나게 [hu-beol-na-gae] literally "dreadfully" (in Jeolla dialect), meaning eagerly as in when you eat spicy food, you have to eat faster and faster.

이빠이

[i-bba-i]

fill 'er up (at a gas station)

가득, 충분함을 의미하는 일본어로부터 유래된 이 표현은 한국인들에 의해 기름을 가득 넣고 싶은 경우 쓰여지고 있다. 또한 '많이', '아주 많은' 등의 의미로 다른 상황에서도 쓰여진다.

From the Japanese for "enough," this expression has been borrowed by Koreans to indicate that one wants to fill up their gas tank and can also be used in other situations to mean "a lot" or "very many."

Synonym: 만땅 [mang-ddang] fill to the brim.

콩글리쉬 대화

ChangHyun 오라이, 오라이, 오라이... 웁스, 빠꾸 빠꾸. 오케바리.

Peter 창현아, 여기서 뭐해? 너 호프에서 일하지 않았었어?

ChangHyun 아, 이거 새로운 아르바이트야. 이빠이?

Peter 어, 가득! 내 말은, 그래, 이빠이.

ChangHyun 쌩유. 바이 바이.

Peter 화이팅.

Conversations in Konglish

창현 Orai, orai, orai... Oops, baku baku. OK buddy.

피터 ChangHyun, what are you doing here?
Weren't you working at a hopeu (hof)...

창현 Ah, this is my new arbeit. Ibbai?

피터 OK, fill 'er up! I mean, yeah, ibbai.

창현 Saengyu. Bai bai.

피터 Hwai-ting.

Konglish 101

Eng-eu-rish for the Masses

콩글리쉬 101

- **air-con** 에어콘 air conditioner
- **a-pa-teu** 아파트 apartment
- **a-reu-ba-i-teu** 아르바이트 a part-time job, from the German arbeit for work, these days, also called alba 알바, which could be related to Koreans' love for Jessica Alba.
- **bba-ggu** 빠꾸 an instruction to "back up" a car. From the Japanese *baku*.
- **ho-peu** 호프 a bar or pub, from the German 'Hof.' Actually, this is merely the Korean mispronunciation of Hof as there is no equivalent to an 'f' in Korean.
- **hwa-i-ting** 화이팅 literally "fighting." This oft-cited Konglish word has no English equivalent. It is an interjection used to express a healthy "fighting" spirit or tenacity of will. Its closest English equivalents might be: "Right on!," "Go for it!," "Get it done!" ("Git'er done!"), "Don't give up!" etc.
- **MT** 엠티 literally "Membership Training" which refers to a weekend drinking getaway with people from the same major or sometimes coworkers.
- **ok bu-ddy** 오케바리 that's sounds good or let's do that.
- **o-ra-i o-ra-i** 오라이 오라이 for all right, all right when backing up a car
- **o-to-bai** 오토바이 "autobike" for a motorcycle
- **P-turn** 피턴 many intersections in Korea do not allow left turns, so it is often necessary to do a P-turn immediately after an intersection, taking a right at the first alley, then two more rights to achieve a 'P' directionally.
- **remote con** 리모콘 a remote control.
- **same same** 쌤쌤 slang for "the same" when comparing two things.
- **seu-kin** 스킨 toner as in "I put on my *skin* in the morning."
- **ssang-yu** 쌩유 thank you (in Korean rapper form).
  Also: ssang-kyu 쌩큐, **ssang-yu-bae-ri-kam-sa** 쌩유베리감사 combining "thank you very…" & Korean "thank you," **ssang-yu** 쌩유베리망치 thank you very much (making "much" sound like the Korean word for "hammer")
- **te-re-bi** 테레비 television (this is a bit outdated, but some still use it).
- **wa-i-sya-sseu** 와이샤쓰 an oxford, button-down or dress shirt, from the English "white shirt."

입이 싸다

[ib-i ssa-da]

loose-tongued; can't keep a secret; a blabbermouth

비속어로 자주 쓰이는 관용어로서, 글자 그대로 풀이하면 입이 싸다라는 뜻. 입이 가벼워 비밀을 지키지 않는 것으로 비슷한 영어표현으로는 "loose tongued"가 있다.

Literally "your mouth is cheap." This expression is often used as slang when talking about someone who can't keep a secret. Some American English synonyms would be "a big mouth" or "a gossip monger," but its closest equivalent is "loose tongued."

숨은 뜻

JiYoon	여보세요.
SoYoon	응... 〔어...〕
JiYoon	너 왜 그렇게 입이 싸?!
SoYoon	으? 〔무슨 소리야?〕
JiYoon	내 새 남자친구한테 코 고친거 다 말했잖아... 입이 싼 년!
SoYoon	음. 〔어. 그랬지 – 그래서 어쩌라고?〕
JiYoon	걔 고친 여자 싫어한다면서 나 버렸단 말이야!!
SoYoon	응, 흠. 끊어. 〔어, 니 등에 칼 꽂았다 이년아! 그래서 뭐. 안녕.〕

The Subtext

지윤	Hello.
소윤	Eung... [Yes...]
지윤	Why are you so ibi ssa?!
소윤	Uh? [What do you mean?]
지윤	You told my new boyfriend about my nose job... You ibi ssan bitch!
소윤	Mm. [Yep. I did – and so what?]
지윤	He said he hates girls that have been cut and he dumped me!!
소윤	Eung. Hm. Geunneo. [Yep, I'm a backstabbing bitch! So what. Bye.]

Korean Phone Language and Etiquette

- **여보세요** [yo-bo-sae-yo] hello on the phone. Literally means "look here," and sounds to foreigners like "excuse me?" as if it means "why are you bothering me?" but it just means hello.

- **어디세요** [o-di-sae-yo] literally "where are you," but actually means what company are you calling from, who are you, or for what reason are you calling. This is most often used at a place of business.

- **끊어** [geunh-eo] literally meaning "cut off." This curt expression is used to finish a conversation and effectively say goodbye on the phone.

The Odd Sounds of a Cellphone

- **어** [uh] a lazyman's "yes." An affirmation similar to the English *mmm*. Some Koreans will answer their mobile phone and have an entire conversation with only this word, then end with the terse *geunheo* (끊어).

- There are many variations: 응, 으, 음, 흠 [eung, eu, eum, heum]. These sounds are all used similarly to carry on a conversation without actually saying anything. The various meanings can be inferred from the intonation.

  1. These sounds can be slightly altered to fain cuteness (only used by girls), as in 앙, 웅, 힝 [ang, ung, hing] or the longer 우우우웅 [u-u-u-ung].

  2. It may also show that the speaker doesn't have much interest in talking.

  3. It is very common among cheaters or just as a way to avoid saying anything that might be heard by others around you (read – **양다리** [yang-da-ri] two-timing cheaters).

  4. It can also be used to simply indicate that you are still listening to the speaker, though maybe not so actively engaged in the conversation.

- **콜** [uh] a quick and clear affirmation similar to "sure" or "you bet." (Can be used in person as well.)

잉여

[ing-yeo]

a useless human being; a waste of space

다소 백수의 표현과 비슷한 의미이다. 이는 누군가 직업이 없고, 인생에서 아무것도 성취한 것이 없다고 느낄 때 자기 스스로를 비하하는 말이다. 혹은 쓸모 없이 잉여시간을 보내고 있는 사람에게 어느 정도 빈정대는 의미로 쓰이기도 한다.

Somewhat similar to a *baeksu*, this is a self-deprecating term for someone who has no job and feels like they are not accomplishing anything with their life. *Ingyeo* is also used as a somewhat sarcastic term about a person with surplus time that is considered useless, literally "a leftover."

냉동상

SaengTae	명태, 요즘 어떻게 지냈어?
MyongTae	뭐 계속 신선하고 맛있는 상태로 있으려 노력 중이지. 넌?
SaengTae	항상 있던 저녁 식사 테이블에서 양념 듬뿍 받고 있어.
MyongTae	노가리나 동태는 요즘 어떻대?
SaengTae	노가리는 호프집에서 사람들 배 채워주며 그럭저럭 잘 지내는 것 같아.
MyongTae	동태는?
SaengTae	냉동실 뒤편에 처박혀 잉여처럼 있지 뭐.
MyongTae	아 그래, 걔는 거기에 너무 오래 숨어있으면서 인생을 다 허비하고 있는 것 같아.

Freezer Burn

생태	MyeongTae, what have you been up to lately?
명태	Just trying to stay fresh and delicious. And you?
생태	At my usual place on the dinner table getting all spiced up.
명태	Have you seen NoGari or DongTae?
생태	NoGari is hangin' in the hofs, feeding the masses.
명태	And DongTae?
생태	Stuck in the back of the freezer like the ingyeo he is.
명태	Yeah, he's been hiding there so long, he's burned his life away.

The Straight Scoop

Feeling Fishy?
The characters in the conversation above are personified fish.

MyeongTae [명태] is an Alaskan Pollack
SaengTae [생태] is 'fresh' Alaskan Pollack
NoGari [노가리] is a young Alaskan Pollack (most often eaten dried as a side dish with alcohol, like little dried minnows to dip in spicy pepper paste)
DongTae [동태] is frozen Alaskan Pollack

임마

[i m - m a]

you little so-and-so; you little bastard

이 약한 욕은 영어표현 "야 너 (죄그만 녀석)"와 닮아있다. 이 표현에는 듣는 사람을 얕보고 있음이 드러난다. 원래 '인마'에서 유래되었으며 흔히 친한 친구 사이에서 "너, 뭐냐?"의 의미를 포함하며, 혹은 낯선 사람과 다툴 때 그들을 낮춰 부르는 말로도 쓰인다.

This soft swear is similar to the English "you little… " (with an ending like "shit" or "so-and-so") and implies that the person being referred to is small and insignificant compared to the speaker. Originally *inma* (인마), it is commonly used by an elder (a parent, uncle or grandparent), between friends in jest, to express "what the fuck," or it can be used to talk down to a stranger to start a fight.

후유증

DongWon   오, 너무 어지러워. 나 죽을것 같아.

TaeYong   임마, 내가 위스키하고 와인 섞어먹지 말랬잖아.

WonDong   엄마, 나 차라리 죽고싶어.

TaeYong   엄마는 도와주지 않을거야, 임마…

내 차에 토하면 내 손으로 죽여버리겠어.

The Aftermath

동원   Ohhhh, I'm so dizzy. I'm gonna die.

태용   Imma, I told you never to mix whisky and wine.

동원   Mama, I wanna die.

원동   Mama isn't going to help you, Imma…

You puke in my car and I'll kill you myself.

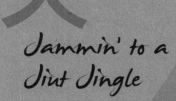

Jammin' to a Jiut Jingle

To jaw the j right,

      just tip your tongue up and mingle it

with a jab forward in the jazzy night.

            Don't jabber on, just aspirate it.

      J's judgeless, so don't equate it

        with any other letter and yet

it's as close to a Z as Korean can get.

        What's that? gg 지지 you say?

          Fear not. The good game can continue

            as the jingle returns to J.

작업

[jag-eop]

to pick up; mack on; go to work on

군대 내에서의 의무적인 잡역, 일을 뜻하는 말로, 일터에서 프로젝트(일)를 행함에 있어서 자주 사용되지만 비속어로는 실패의 위험 속에서 데이트를 하기 위해 상대를 꼬시려고 노력하는 행위를 의미한다. 비슷한 영어표현: going to work on someone.

Literally for "fatigue duty" in the army or conducting an operation, this expression is often used in Korean society for doing a project at work. *Jakeop* became slang for picking someone up due the effort it requires and possibly the danger of failure. Similar to the English "going to work on someone." A man who is good at *jakeop* is a *jakeop nom* (작업놈) a philandering, flirtatious bastard.

여자들 파내기

SunSu	너 어디 가는거야?
PaRam	어디든 바람 부는데로…
SunSu	오, 지금 저 여자 말하는거지? 너 작업 걸려고?
	하지만, 저 여자를 얻으려면 선수와 같은 힘과 기술이 필요할거야.
PaRam	아니지, 작업을 위해서는 휙 부는 바람과 같이 빠르게 덮치고,
	산들바람으로 그녀의 뺨을 살짝 스친 뒤, 부드러운 목소리로
	그녀의 귀에 속삭여야 하는거야.
KwangSung	작업에 대해 얘기한거야? 아니, 아니지. 너네들은 두려움부터
	없애야해 죽음 혹은 실패에 대한. 그리고 삽은 언제나 챙기고.

Digging up girls

선수	Where are you going?
바람	Whichever way the wind blows …
선수	Oh, I see her now. You're going to do jageop, but to get her you'll need strength and skill like an athlete.
바람	No, for jageop I'll just swoop in on a gust of air, caress her cheek with a soft breeze and whisper gentle nothings in her ear.
광성	Did you say jageop? No, no. You boys need to have no fear of death or failure, and always bring your shovel.

Dating Box I

Gettin' Jiggy with It

- **소개팅** [so-gae-ting]

Sogae is to introduce someone and the "ting" comes from "meeting" to mean a blind date which extremely popular in with Koreans of both sexes.

Variations on sogaeting:

미팅 [mi-ting] meeting, usually a group blind date with three or more guys and girls.

점팅 [jeom-ting] lunch meeting

폰팅 [pon-ting] phone meeting

문자팅 [mun-ja-ting] text meeting

번개팅 [beon-gae-ting] a sudden meeting

헌팅 [hun-ting] hunting for girls, chasing tail

- **부킹** [booking]

Common practice in South Korean nightclubs, *booking* describes a type of forced socialization between two genders. First, *bikkis* (삐끼) in front of the club cajole attractive women inside where as soon as they sit, waiters grab them by the wrist and drag them to another table to sit with men. If they are interested, they stay, and if the men are interested they offer them a drink. This process of forcibly dragging Korean females over to meet men is time tested and admittedly effective in a society that is largely reserved and reluctant to approach others. *Booking* is not only sanctioned by the club, but requested of waiters who expect a tip for *booking* well and though some see the service as forced and potentially illicit, to others it is deemed necessary as:

a) Koreans have traditionally been too shy to approach strangers of their own volition; **b)** Korea lacks Western-style bars where people can routinely socialize with strangers; **c)** Korean-style drinking establishments are populated by booths and tables that cater to couples or groups of friends who, generally, do not mingle easily with outsiders.

잘 나가

[jal na-ga]

on a roll; to go well or get on (with women)

단순히 잘 하고 있음을 의미, 혹은 질문으로 일은 잘 진행되는지를 물을 때 쓰인다. 비속어로는 다른 성과의 원만한 관계의 의미를 내포하며, 비슷한 영어표현으로는 "How they hangin?" 혹은 "You getting any?"가 있다. 이는 또한 매우 인기있거나 성공했을 때에도 쓰일 수 있다.

Simply meaning "to do well," or in a question, "are you doing well?" The slang implies getting on with the opposite sex, similar to the American expressions, "how they hangin'?" or "you getting any?" This can also relate to a person being popular, professionally or otherwise.

배트맨 카

Robin	그래 어제는 어떻게 됐냐? 잘 나가?
Batman	배트맨 카? 물론이지, 잘 달리고 말고.
Robin	배트맨 카 안에서? 누구 태웠는데?
Batman	캣우먼 태워줬지.
Robin	워우. 너 정말 굉장하구나.
Batman	허? 나 말고, 전부 배트맨 카에 대한거였는데... 잘 간다고. 완전 잘 나가

The Batmobile

로빈	So how did it go last night? Jalnaga?
배트맨	The Batmobile? Sure, it rides great.
로빈	In the Batmobile? Who did you ride?
배트맨	I gave Catwoman a ride.
로빈	Wow. You really are stupendous.
배트맨	Huh? It's not me, it's all the Batmobile ... It drives well. Really jalnaga!

쥐뿔

[jui-bbol]

it aint shit; something trivial or insignificant

글자 그대로는, 쥐의 고환(불알)을 뜻한다. 이 표현은 "너는 아무것도(쥐의 불알에 대해서 조차 – 혹은 그런 가치없는 것들) 몰라"를 의미하는 "너는 쥐뿔도 모른다"와 같이 부정적으로 사용된다.

Literally "a rat's balls." This expression is usually used in the negative as in "You don't even know *juibbol*," meaning: "You don't know Jack" (not even about a rat's balls – or other trivial or insignificant things).

뿔난 쥐?

Siwoo 쥐뿔을 글자 그대로 해석하면 쥐의 뿔을 뜻하는 것 같아.

Peter 뭐? 넌 쥐뿔도 모르냐? 뿔은 고환(불알)을 말하는 거잖아.

       쥐한테 빌어먹을 뿔 같은게 어딨어.

Siwoo 오, 그렇네.

Peter 그래, 니가 지난번에 이게 불알을 뜻한다고 했어.

Siwoo 그래 알아. 보잘 것 없이 너무나도 작고 하찮은 것. 쥐뿔 몰라?

       난 그냥 농담한거라고!!

Horned Rats?

시우 I think *juibbol* is literally a rat's horn.

피터 What? Don't you even know *juibbol*? Bbol means ball or balls.

      A rat doesn't have any fucking horns.

시우 Oh, really.

피터 Yeah, you told me it meant balls last time.

시우 Of course, so small they're insignificant. Don't you know *juibbol*?

      I was just kidding!!

쥐꼬리만큼

[chui-ggo-ri man-keum]

just a bit; a meager amount; fuck all

이 표현은 아주 적은 양 또는 거의 없음을 의미한다. 영어의 "a pittance," "peanuts," "chicken feed"와 같이 대부분 적은 월급에 대한 불만을 풍자적으로 얘기할 때 사용하지만 바라는 양보다 적은 양을 가리키는 어느 경우에라도 사용할 수 있다.

Literally meaning "as much as a rat's tail," this expression is equivalent to "a measly amount" or "hardly at all." Most often used sarcastically in reference to receiving an unsatisfactory salary, it is similar to "a pittance," "peanuts," or "chicken feed," but can be used for anything that is smaller than a desired amount.

서울에서의 또 다른 쥐꼬리

[서울에서 택시에 타며]

Peter	이태원이요.
Taxi Driver	와우! 한국말 잘하시네요.
Peter	네? 제가 "요"라고 말해서요?
Taxi Driver	발음이 정말 좋아요.
Peter	아니요, 아니요. 쥐꼬리만큼밖에 못 해요.
Taxi Driver	와하하하. 그 표현은 어디서 배웠어요?
Pete	음.. 글쎄요. 공부 열심히 했죠, 길거리에서요.
Taxi Driver	하하. 음.. 제 월급은 쥐꼬리만큼이에요.
Peter	네. 제 월급도요.

The Batmobile

[getting into a random taxi in Seoul]

피터   Itaewon please.

택시기사   Wow? You speak Korean so well?

피터   What? Just because I gave it a "yo" ending?

택시기사   Your pronunciation is perfect.

피터   No, no, no. I can only speak chuiggori mankeum.

택시기사   Wha-ha-ha-ha. How did you learn that expression?

피터   Ummm, well. Studied hard, studied in the street.

택시기사   Ha ha. Well, my salary is chuiggori mankeum.

피터   Yeah. Mine too.

Just a bit

The many ways of expressing how 'little' you have!

- 개미똥만큼 [gae-mi-dong-man-keum] as much as an ant's poop
- 코딱지만큼 [ko-ddak-ji-man-keum] as much as a booger (dried nasal mucus)
- 눈곱만큼 [noon-geop-man-keum] as much as 'sleep' in your eyes (crusty mucus in the corner of your eye usually upon waking)
- 귀밥만큼 [gui-bab-man-keum] as much as earwax
- 새발의 피만큼 [sae-bal-e pi man-keum] as much as a blood from a bird's claw

지못미

[ji-mot-mi]

sorry I didn't get your back

이 표현은 사실 '지켜주지 못해 미안해'의 약자이다. 이것은 특별히 공인인 배우들, 모델들, 가수들, 혹은 다른 유명인사들에게 쓰인다. 이들이 부정적인 것(파파라치, 못된 괴롭힘, 비밀스런 과거 사진 유출 등)으로 부터 상처를 입을 때 팬들이 온라인상에서 쓰는 말이다.

This expression is actually an acronym for *ji-kyo-ju-ji mot-hae mi-an-hae* (지켜주지 못해 미안해), which means "I'm sorry I couldn't protect you." Used especially by fans for actors & actresses, models, singers and others in the public eye. Fans write *jimotmi* online when someone famous is hurt by harmful or damaging acts (paparazzi, bad press, nasty comments, when compromising pictures are released online, etc.)

'올드보이' 온라인 팬 클럽

Arum   방가 방가 민식, 나 니가 딸이랑 잔 기사 봤어.

그건 사실이 아닌데... 지못미!

HanSum   나도... 나랑 자기전에는 안돼지... 크, 크!

Kaeul   민식 오빠, 오빠랑 오빠 딸 사진 나와버린거야? 지못미!

난 파파라치가 싫어! OTL

YuJa   왜 걔들은 항상 널 괴롭히는거니? 지못미! 그게 뭐 어때서.

너가 니 딸이랑 키스했다면...

나랑도 언제든 키스 할 수 있는거잖아.

전화해. 010-910-2234!

나의 메시지를 씹지 말라!!

JiTae   으이구, 불쌍한 놈... KIN

The Straight Scoop

으이구 [eu-i-gu] poor you. Equivalent to the Korean expression *igo* (아이고). *Igo*, meaning "oh my," "good gracious" or "woe is me," would be used as a type of sigh or expression of frustration or surprise to oneself. The *euigu* however, would be used for another person (not oneself) as with the English "poor baby." It can also be used as a sound of satisfaction, similar to "whew."

'Old Boy' Fan Club Chatroom

아름	Bangga bangga MinShik, I saw the posting about you sleeping with your daughter. I know it's not true … jimotmi!
한숨	Me too … I know you're saving yourself for me … kh, kh!
가을	MinShik oppa, the pictures of you and her just came out? Jimotmi! I hate the paparazzi! OTL
유자	Why are they always bothering you? Jimotmi! So what if you kiss your daughter … you can kiss me anytime. Call me 010-910-2234! Don't sshibta my message!
지태	Eu-i-gu, poor baby … KIN

Text Box

The Basics of Korean Texting

- **감사감사** [gam-sa-gam-sa] "Thanks, thanks."
- **뭥미** [mueong-mi] similar in sound to mueoni (뭐니) what's your problem? but the impression is stronger, like "what the hell is your problem?"
- **방가방가** [bang-ga-bang-ga] "Great to meet you!" (considered comical for its abridged repetition)
- **삐까삐까** [bbi-gga-bbi-gga] "Same same."
- **씹다** [ssib-da] "Why are you eating my text?" (not answering me)
- **열공** [yeol-gong] from yeolshimhi gongbu (열심히 공부) "Study hard!"
- **즐겜** [jeul-game] "It was a good game."
- **지지** [G-G] "GG" for Good game.
- **OTL** (online) "A breakdown or collapse." OTL actually Looks like someone on their hands and knees crying.
- **KIN** Looks like the Korean jeul (즐) on its side, and originated from **즐겜** [jeul-game], but came to mean piss off, go away or shut up.
- **ㄱㅅ** (Thank You) is just a combination of the first two letters of "**감사**" which means thank you.

진도 어디까지 나갔어?

[jin-do eo-di-gga-ji na-gass-eo]

how far did you get (with him/her)?

글자 그대로는, 수업을 얼마만큼 했는지 묻는 말. 이 비속어는 누군가에게 이성과의 교제에 있어서 어느 정도의 성적/데이트의 진행이 이루어졌는지를 물을 때 쓰인다. 이 표현은 다소 노골적이며, 같은 영어식 표현으로는 "몇 루까지 나갔어?"가 있다. 이 영어식 표현에서 1루는 키스, 2루는 상반신, 3루는 하반신, 그리고 홈런은 상대방과 갈 때까지 갔음을 의미한다.

Literally "how much did you progress," and related to studies (as in till what page, or up to which lesson). *Jindo eodiggaji nagasseo* is used to ask about someone's dating or sexual progress with an intended partner. It is rather crude, and roughly equivalent to an American asking "What base did you get to?"

과외 수업

SeungMan	너 어제 나이트 가지 않았어? 진도 어디까지 나갔어?
DooHwan	네, 맞습니다. 어제 수업 받았죠...
SeungMan	정오까지 진도 보고서 가지고 와.
DooHwan	저의 만남에 관한? 그건 그저 "과외수업"이었을 뿐이었는데... 더 이상 묻지 말아주십시오.
SeungMan	난 구체적인 모든걸 알고싶어. 진도 어디까지 나갔어?
DooHwan	알겠어요, 알겠습니다. 밤새 "공부"해서 "책 한권 다 끝냈어요." 하 하!
SeungMan	일본 대사하고?! 그 사람한테서 뭘 배웠냐고!
DooHwan	어어~. 글쎄요, 선생님. 여자들하고 너무 바빴기 때문에 아... 그 상황에 대한 이야기는 하지못했지만, 정은 엄청 들었습니다.
SeungMan	(화나 보인다)
DooHwan	당장 그 여자를..아니 일을 착수 하겠습니다.

Private Lessons

승만   You went to the 'night' last night, didn't you?
      Jindo eodiggaji nagasseo?

두환   Yeah, I learned a lesson all right...

승만   I want a progress report on my desk by noon.

두환   About my encounter? It was a "private" lesson...
      I don't kiss and tell.

승만   I want to know all the details. Jindo eodiggaji nagasseo?

두환   OK, OK. We "studied" all night and "finished the book." Ha ha!

승만   I mean with the Japanese Ambassador?!
      What did you learn from him?

두환   Ohhhhhh. Well, sir. We were so busy with the girls, we never
      talked about the a ... the situation, but we've got mad jeong now.

승만   [Looks angry]

두환   I'll get right on her, I mean ... on it, sir!

The Straight Scoop

정(情) [jeong] literally a warmth that builds up between people over time and is
indicative of an old, trusted and welcome friend.

짝퉁

[jjak-tung]

a knockoff; black market merchandise

짝은 무익한 것 혹은 아무짝에도 쓸모없음을, 그리고 퉁은 낮은 질의 놋쇠를 의미한다. 이 두 글자가 합쳐지면 하찮은 놋쇠를 뜻하여, 비속어로는 간단히 모조한것, 특별히 유명 브랜드 상품의 이미테이션을 말할 때 쓰인다.

The *jjak* (짝) refers to something useless or "good for nothing," and *tung* (퉁) means "low quality brass." The combination refer to a brass trinket and as slang it simply suggests something fake, particularly an knockoff of a name brand product. Not necessarily of poor quality like *heojeop* (허접).

Synonyms: 짭퉁 [jjab-tung] impure brass & 짜가 [jja-ga] a reversal of 가짜 [ga-jja] meaning fake or imitation & 야매 [ya-mae] a bootleg product.

B-브랜드 쇼핑

HeeYeon 그거 진짜 구찌야? 아니면, 이태원 표 짝퉁?

Minji 이게 짜가로 보여? 내가 그런 짭퉁을 살 사람으로 보이냐고?!
감히 어떻게 나에게!!

HeeYeon 그냥 한 말이야. 단지 네가 좋은 가격에 샀나 궁금해서.
나도 가끔 짝퉁 사거든...

MinJi 농담이야. 사실 이거 짝퉁이야. 내가 가지고 있는 유일한 진퉁은
남자친구가 사준거거든. 하도 애원하길래 받아줬지.
이거 얼마주고 샀는지 맞춰봐...

B-Brand Shopping

회연 Is that a real Gucci? Or an Itaewon jjaktung?

민지 Does it look jjaga? Do I look like someone who would buy
jjabtung?! How dare you!!

회연 I didn't mean anything. Just wondered if you got a good deal. I
buy jjaktung sometimes ...

민지 Just kidding. It's jjaktung. The only real stuff I have, I let my
boyfriends buy for me (after much cajoling). Guess how much I
got it for ...

194

짱이다
[jjang-i-da]

it's the tops; it's cool; it's the bomb

짱은 무리의 대장, 우두머리를 나타내는 말로 그만큼 멋짐, 훌륭함을 의미하게 되었다. 다른 비슷한 표현으로는, 캡이다, 캡숑, 그리고 가장 최근에 생겨난 '킹왕짱'과 '님 좀 짱인듯'이 있다.

Jjang, the head or leader of a group, came to express approval or describe something that is "pretty damn great." Some similar expressions are *kapida* (캡이다 – ace, it's cap, it's the best), *kapshong* (캡숑 – better than the best), and most recently, *king-wangjjang* (킹왕짱 – king, king *jjang*) and *nim jom jjangindeut* (님 좀 짱인듯 – you look a bit *jjang*). English equivalents – cool, fresh, with it, the shit, the bomb, etc.

바보의 기회

ByungShik	너 어디가냐?
KwangSung	나 이태원에서 알바 구했어…
ByungShik	와우, 님 좀 짱인듯! 제시카 알바 보는거야? 걔 짱이야.
KwangSung	아니, 일자리 구했다고. 이태원에 알바로.
ByungShik	이태원에 온데? 캡이다. 나 가도 돼?
KwangSung	아니, 얼간이! 알바. 아르바이트.
ByungShik	오 이런 일이! 너 제시카랑 같이 일 하는거야? 캡숑이다.
KwangSung	알았다, 알았어. 알바보러 오고 싶어? 주유소에 있어.

Brush with Fame

병식	Where are you going?
광성	I've got an alba in Itaewon …
병식	Wow, nim jom jjangindeut! You're going to see Jessica Alba? She's jjangida.
광성	No. I've got a part time job, in Itaewon, an alba.
병식	She's coming to Itaewon? Kapida. Can I come?
광성	No, stupid! Alba. It's an arbeit!!
병식	Oh my god! You get to work with Jessica? Kapshong!
광성	OK, OK. You want to come see alba? It's at the gas station.

짬뽕

[jjam-bbong]

a person of mixed blood; mulatto or half-breed

보통, 짬뽕이라고 하면 매운 해물이 섞여있는 국수를 뜻한다. 그러나 비속어로서의 이것은 혼혈인을 뜻하게 된다. 이것은 경멸적인 용어로 다른 인종과의 혼혈을 보고 한국인들이 사용하는 표현이다.

Normally, *jjambbong* is a spicy mixed seafood and noodle dish available at Korean style Chinese restaurants and as slang can be used for anything that is mixed. It is however, often used as to belittle someone of mixed racial heritage, and in particular for biracial Koreans. Depending on the tone, it's connotation can range from simply insensitive to disparaging or a racial slur.

섞인 축복

Ajumma1   그 소식 들었어? 승만이가 외국인이랑 결혼했대!

Ajumma2   어, 그 여자 오스트리아 귀족이래.

Ajumma1   근데, 아이들은 어쩌니? 걔네는 짬뽕 일거야!

Ajumma2   애들은 분명히 이쁠거야.
            지금이 니 생각과 마음을 고쳐먹을 때야.

A Mixed Blessing

아줌마1   Did you hear the news? Seungman married a foreigner!

아줌마2   Yeah, I hear she's an Austrian aristocrat.

아줌마1   But what if they have kids? They'll be jjambbong!

아줌마2   I bet they'll be beautiful. Maybe it's time you opened up your
            mind... and your heart.

More 'Mixed' Metaphors

튀기 [tui-gi] of mixed blood, a mongrel or half-breed (originally a crossbreed of a donkey and a cow and extremely offensive).

혼혈아 [hon-hyeol-a] a child of mixed racial origins. While commonly used in Korea and not pejorative, it's English equivalent (mixed) would be somewhat rude or even offensive to some (better to say 1/2 Korean or of biracial parentage).

Intolerance, Prejudice & Xenophobia... Oh my!

Racial Epithets for the Ethnically Unempathetic

Despite the fact that Korea has people of many ethnic backgrounds, and has intermixed with the Chinese, Japanese, and Mongolians throughout its long history, some continue to look down on others. People of mixed blood have historically been subjected to beating and ridicule (especially in schools), and though this attitude is becoming less and less common in recent years, there is still an element that is too intolerant to other ethnicities.

- 외국놈 [oi-gug-nom] foreign bastard (derogatory for any non-native)

- 쪽바리 [jjog-ba-ri] an ethnic slur for a Japanese person, like "Jap"

- 양키 [yang-ki] or 양놈 [yang-nom] yankee bastard or fuckin' westerner

- 미국놈[mi-gug-nom] an American bastard

- 코쟁이 [ko-jang-i] a (big) nosed fanatic – meaning Westerner (like cracker)

- 깜둥이 [ggam-deung-i] black one (similar to the offensive English, nigger)

- 검둥이 [geom-deung-i] black one (not quite as offensive as *ggamdeungi*)

- 사악한 검은 원숭이 [bbal-gang-i] a wicked black monkey, recently used in a North Korean press release to describe president Obama.

- 짱깨 [jjang-ggae] pejorative for a Chinese person, similar to "chink" as it relates to the Korean Chinese dish 자장면 [ja-jjang-myeon], or a *jajang-myun* delivery man, which is considered a very low position.

- 빨갱이 [bbal-gang-i] fuckin' commie (derogatory for a North Korean)

(Though we catalog these insults and epithets here, we only do so in the interest of understanding, in the potential offered by a complete education of both the good and bad, and in hopes that you will never use them yourself.)

짭새

[jjab-sae]

the pigs, the fuzz; police (derogatory)

문자그대로는 상스러운, 잡종 새를 뜻한다. 비속어로서는 섞인, 순수하지 않은 것을 의미하는 잡과 비슷한 짭이라는 글자와 조류, 더 나아가서는 이리저리 옮겨다니며 지저귀는 새와 같은 위반단속을 하는 사람들을 연상캐하는 새라는 글자가 합쳐져 경찰을 의미한다. 이는 거의 젊은 세대들에 의해 사용되어지고 비슷한 영어식 표현으로는 'pig'가 있다.

Literally "a vulgar, mixed-breed bird." *Jjab* (짭), similar to *jab* (잡) is a mixed, or impure thing, and *sae* (새) most likely refers to a bird or fowl, or more particularly the annoying chirping of a bird as the officer wanders from place to place like a bird ticketing people. This insult is used mostly by youth and is roughly equivalent to the English insult to police: "the pigs."

짭새가 날아든다!

ChangHyun	(음주단속 후) 나는 저런 짭새새끼가 싫어. 저놈은 시민들 괴롭히는 것 말고는 할게 없대? 지 주제를 알아야지!
ByungShik	야! 너 네가 깡이 세다고 하지 않았었어? 얼굴 마주보고 짭새라고 해보지 그래? 넌 군인이고 쟨 기껏해야 경찰이야.
ChangHyun	지금 나보고 겁쟁이라는거야? 잠깐... 야, 짭새야!
Police Officer	(경찰이 차 쪽으로 다시 걸어온다) 뭐라고?
ChangHyun	아, 그냥 노래에요 – 라디오에서 나온... "짭새가 날아든다!"
Police Officer	차에서 내려…

Jjabsae, fly over here!

창현	(After sobriety test) I hate that kind of jjabsae SOB. Doesn't he have anything better to do than bother citizens? He should know his place!
병식	I thought you said you were brave! Why didn't you call him jjabsae to his face? You outrank him.
창현	You calling me a coward? Watch this ... Ya, Jjabsae ya!
경찰	[Cop walks back to car] What did you say?
창현	Ah, just singing – it was on the radio ... "Jjabsae, fly over here!"
경찰	Get out of the car …

Swear Box

Some say this is the first stuff you should learn…
We say that too!

Be careful!! Shhh! Don't say these, but you should know what they mean…
especially if you are watching gangster movies… Korean Swearing in brief:

The basics

DANGER!

- 년 [nyeon] bitch
- 놈 [nom] bastard (pejorative for a man)
- 좆 [jot] dick or cock
- 개 [gae] dog or cur (used in combination with other offensive language)
- 개새끼 [gae-sae-ggi] SOB – son of a bitch (literally "a dog's offspring") or 개새 [gae-sae] for short
- 씨발 [ssi-bal] similar to "you fucking (so-and-so)" in English, but literally meaning "you will sell your seed." This can be shortened to 씹 [sshib]
- 쌍 [ssang] low-born or ignoble from Chosun dynasty or before, also 쌍 [sshyang] most often used as a combination 쌍놈 [ssang-nom] low bastard
- 미친 [mi-chin] crazy, most often used as a combination 미친새끼 [mi-chin sae-ggi] crazy SOB, 미친년 [mi-chin nyeon] crazy bitch, or 미친놈 [mi-chin nom] crazy bastard

The body parts – the unmentionables and offenders
Sex organs

- 보지 [bo-ji] slang for vulva muff or pussy, also 뽕 [bbong] or 잠지 [jam-ji]
- 자지 [ja-ji] penis or dick, similar to 좆 [jot] cock, or
- 고추 [go-chu] literally "a pepper," but childish slang for a penis as with peepee or weewee.
- 젖 [jeot] breast or breast milk, also 젖가슴 [jeot-ga-seum] boobs or tits
- 젖탱이 [jeot-taeng-i] the cup of the breasts, 찌찌 [jji-jji] breast (somewhat childish)
- 유두 [yu-du] nipples or 젖꼭지 [jeot-ggok-ji] literally, the breast spigot

쩐다

[jjeon-da]

tight; kickass; (sometimes awful)

쩐다는 많은 상황에서 쓰일 수 있다; 이는 때때로 나쁜 의미로 사용될 수도 있지만, 주로 무언가 아주 멋지고 굉장한 경우에 사용되는 표현이다. 영어 슬랭 tight와 비슷하다. 아마도 적응한다는 뜻의 북한 방언 절다에서 유래된 것으로 보인다. 미국 해병대의 "되게 하여, 적응하고 극복하라." 라는 말과 같이 누군가 어떠한 것에 잘 적응한다면, 곧 능숙해지고 이는 아주 굉장한 수준이 되게 된다; 쩐이다!

Jjeonda can be used in many situations; it can occasionally be used for something bad, but it is most often used for something that is wonderful or awesome – similar to the American slang, tight. Most likely taken from the North Korean dialect, *jeolda* (절다) means to adapt. Like with the USMC's "Improvise, Adapt and Overcome," if one adapts well, they become so adept at it, it's powerfully awesome; it kicks ass!

개 쩐다

Robin	어이쿠, 새로운 장치네. 배트맨! 그건 뭐야?
Batman	내 최신 무기야!
Robin	근데 개 목걸이 같이 생겼는데… 고스족이라도 되려고?!
Batman	사실, 이건 배트걸을 위한 거야. 난 단지 시험해보고 있는 중이고.
Robin	와아아아아아우! 이거 개 쩐다! 정말 굉장하네! 완전 쩐다, 배트맨!

Dog-tastic

로빈	Holy, new gadget Batman! What is that?
배트맨	It's my newest weapon!
로빈	But it looks like a dog collar… Are you going goth on us?!
배트맨	Actually, it's for batgirl. I'm just testing it out.
로빈	Wooooow! It's dog-tastic! It's bat-awesome! Totally jjeonda, Batman!

쪽팔리다
[jjok-pal-li-da]

how humiliating; uhhh AWKWARD; to lose face

축어적으로, 얼굴이 팔리다. 이것은 얼굴을 낮게 이르는 말 쪽과 동사 팔리다가 결합되어 생겨난 표현이다. 얼굴 혹은 체면을 잃는것의 느낌은... 부끄러워지는 것.

Literally "your face is sold," this combines the low expression for face (*jjok*) with the verb to be sold (*pallida*). In a sense to lose face or honor, to be shameful or even disgraceful. Similar to one of those mortifying moments when one says "uhhh, AWKWARD!"

족발 잃기

Peter   무슨 말이야. 쪽이 뭔지 모르는거야? 하, 쪽팔리다.

Siwoo   사전에서는 머리를 틀어 올릴 때의 쪽이라는데,

           여자만 해당된대... 내 생각에는 얼굴의 낮춤말 같아.

Peter   음, 어쩌면 일제 강점기에 한국 남자들이 강제로 댕기머리를

           잘라야했던 것 일지도 모르지.

Siwoo   오, 쪽팔려. 모든게 네가 생각하는 역사대로는 아니야.

Peter   창현이한테 전화해서 물어보자.

Siwoo   ㅎㅎ 창현이가 최고 쪽팔린다. 등산하러 가서 족발 먹는게 좋대. 하 하!

Losing Pig's Feet

피터   What do you mean, you don't know what jjok is?
        Huh, jjokpallida.

시우   The dictionary says it's to put one's hair up in a chignon, but that's
        only for a girl ... I think its a low expression for the face.

피터   Well, maybe it's like during the Japanese occupation when Korean
        men were forced to cut their ponytails.

시우   Oh, jjokpallyeo. Not everything is from your history courses.

피터   Call ChangHyun and see what he says ...

시우   He, he. ChangHyun wins the jjokpal contest, he says he likes to eat
        pigs feet (jok bal) when he goes hiking ... Ha ha!

쭉쭉빵빵

[jjuk-jjuk-bbang-bbang]

voluptuous; bootylicious

이 표현은 의태어와 의성어이다. 큰 키와 긴 다리를 나타내는 쭉, 그리고 가득 차 터질것 같은 가슴과 엉덩이를 표현하는 빵빵(빵 터지는 소리 혹은 풍선의 모양)이 결합되었다.

This expression is both mimetic and onomatopoeic. *Jjuk jjuk* (the word for all the way) represents the legs shooting out, and *bbang-bbang* (the sound of popping or the look of a balloon) is for full breasts and buttocks. Booya!

김혜수

JiYoon	오와, 걔 몸 봤어? 휴, 나도 그런 몸매였으면 좋겠다.
Arum	누구, 김혜수? 걔 뚱뚱해!
JiYoon	아니야, 쭉쭉빵빵이지! 나는 왜 쭉쭉빵빵 될 수 없는거지?
Minhee	음, 난 쭉쭉빵빵이야! 그렇게 생각안해?
Arum	장난하냐? 넌 막대기야.
	네 몸에서 곡선이라고는 둥그렇고 큰 얼굴밖에는 없어.
Minhee	내 남자친구가 그랬단말이야!
Arum, JiYoon	(함께 외친다) 바람이가!? 걘 널 침대로 데려가려면 무슨 말이던 할껄!

Kim HyeSu

지윤	My god, did you see her body? Uh, I wish I was like that?
아름	Who, Kim HyeSu? She's fat!
지윤	No, she's jjukjjukbbangbbang! Why can't I be jjukjjukbbangbbang like her?
민희	Well, I'm jjukjjukbbangbbang! Don't you think?
아름	Are you kidding? You're a stick! The only curves you have are in your big round head.
민희	But my boyfriend told me I was!
아름, 지윤	(in unison) PaRam!? He'll say anything to get you into bed!

Get Your Chi Charged

Less lazy than the jùt 尽 above,

    Chiut 尽 gets your Chi charged with love.

Again with the teeth and aspirated to the hilt,

    it can come from charity, but be full of guilt.

      If from an angry girl, chiut chimes

pay attention or forget your rhymes.

착하다

[chak-ha-da]

in good shape; fit; (also affordable: a hot deal)

문자 그대로, 온화하고 상냥한 성격을 뜻한다. 비속어로 착하다는 누군가의 몸매가 좋고 외모가 훌륭하거나, 가격이 저렴한 것을 뜻하게 되었다. "저 여자 정말 착하다."는 실제로 그녀는 섹시하다는 의미이고, "가격이 착하다."는 값이 싸다는 것을 뜻한다.

Literally meaning "good-natured" or "kind-hearted," as slang, *chakhada* has come to mean someone that is sound or in good shape (read – good looking) or something that is reasonably priced. So, "that girl is so kind" would actually mean that she is fit or sexy, and "the price is kind" would mean that it is a hot deal or a good buy.

동종

HanSum	와아아아, 지태는 저어어엉말 착해!
HaPum	뭐?! 우리 같은 영화 본 것 맞아? 걔 완전 나쁜 놈이야!
HanSum	응, 하지만 걔 정말 착하다고!
HaPum	너 미친 것 아니야?
HanSum	나도 그 자식이 나쁜 놈인 것은 알지만, 그래도 정말 잘생겼잖아!
HaPum	아, 그 착하다?! 맞아, 걔 정말 몸매 죽이지.

In Kind

한숨	Wa-a-a, JiTae is soooo chakhae!
하품	What?! Did we see the same movie? He's a total jerk!
한숨	OK, but he's really chakhae!
하품	Have you lost your mind?
한숨	I know he's a jerk, but he's so handsome!
하품	Oh, you mean chakhada! Yeah, he does have a nice bod.

철판깔다
[cheol-pan-ggal-da]

to know no shame; be barefaced or brazen

축어적으로, '너의 얼굴은 철판으로 깔려있다'. 이 관용어는 누군가 체면도 염치도 모르는 채 터무니 없는 말이나 행동을 할 때 강철의 얼굴을 가지고 있는 듯 보임을 반영한다. 부정적인 의미로 자주 사용되지만, 가끔 열심히 영업에 힘쓰고 있는 세일즈맨에게 긍정적인 의미로도 쓰일 수 있다.

Literally "your face is paved with an iron plate." This expression refers to someone who can look steel-faced while saying or doing something incredible, who knows no shame, or simply has no sense of decency. Often used negatively, but can be positive in some situations, as with a hard-dealing salesman with a thick skin.

철판 수로

MyungBak	부산부터 서울까지 대운하를 만들겠어.
DooHwan	농담하냐? 여기는 반도라고!
DaeJung	넌 그저 그런 쓸데 없는 프로젝트로 니 추종자들에게 돈 주려는 거잖아.
MyungBak	난 무슨 일이 있어도 해내고 말겠어… 청계천을 만든 것 처럼.
DooHwan	왜 또 얼굴에 철판깔려고 하는거니?
MyungBak	뭐? 아니야, 난 청계천 위에 있던 철판들도 다 걷어냈는데?

Iron Plated Waterways

명박	I'm going to build a canal from Busan to Seoul.
두환	Are you kidding? This is a peninsula!
대중	You just want to give money to your cronies for a useless project.
명박	I'll get it done no matter what… just like I did with Cheongae Stream.
두환	Why are you doing cheolpanggalda again?
명박	What? No, I took the iron plates off of Cheongae Stream.

찬밥

[chan-bab]

a nobody; an unknown or an upstart

글자 그대로, 차가운 밥. 옛부터 뜨거운 밥은 맛있고 차가운 밥은 쓸모없는 것으로 생각되어져왔다. 이 표현은 관심 받지 못하고 있는, 혹은 누구에게도 중요하지 않은 사람을 의미한다. 비슷한 영어 표현으로는 "get the cold shoulder" 혹은 "yesterday's news"가 있다.

Literally "cold rice." Hot rice is considered delicious, and cold rice useless. This expression suggests someone without a vested interest, or someone of no importance. Distantly related to the English expressions "get the cold shoulder" or "yesterday's news." Can also be used for someone who "wears out their welcome."

찬밥

ChangHyun 나 찬밥 된거야? 며칠 동안 연락도 안되고! 나 차버릴거니?

Arum 아니야, 그저 좀 바빴어…

ChangHyun 바빴다고? 다른 남자들이랑? 다 들었어. 내 제일 친한 친구놈한테
전화하고 둘이서 쇼핑갔다며? 어떻게 네가 그럴 수 있어?
쪽나고 싶어?

Arum 아니야, 깨지고 싶지 않아. 난 정말 널 좋아하니까.
우리 투투데이 때문에 쇼핑한거야. 여기 니 선물!

ChangHyun 뭐? 음, 투투데이? 난, 음, 찬밥 대신 냉면 어때? 하하

Cold Rice

창현 Did I become chanbab? I haven't seen or
heard from you in days! Are you going to kick me to the curb?

아름 No, I've just been busy…

창현 Busy, what? With other guys? I heard you called my best
friend and went shopping with him? How could you?
You want to break up?

아름 I don't want to break up!! I really like you.
I was shopping for our big 22. Here's your present!

창현 What? Um, 22 days? I, um, how about some cold noodles
instead of chanbab? Ha ha.

Dating Box Ⅱ

Keeping Your Dates Straight

- 차다 [cha-da] to dump someone or kick them to the curb.
- 쪽나다 [jjok-na-da] to break up (with each other) also 깨지다 [ggae-ji-da], 끝나다 [ggeut-na-da], and 정리하다 [jeong-ri-ha-da]
- 바람피다 [ba-ram-pi-da] literally "for the wind to blow." This means to be unfaithful in a relationship or cheat on someone .
- 어장관리 [eo-jang-gwan-ri] to (merely pretend to) cultivate potential candidates for a relationship, then dash their hopes (lit. to manage a fish farm).

- 첫눈 [cheot-nun] first snow. The first snow in Korea is important because the word sounds like *cheotnunae banhata* (첫눈에 반하다) which means to fall in love at first sight.
- 빼빼로데이 [bbae-bbae-ro day] 11/11 or Nov. 11th is a day to give your lover *Bbaebbaero,* a brand of chocolate covered pretzels (an amazing marketing scheme of the Lotte group).
- 백일 [baek-il] 100 days. Traditionally, a baby was not named in Korea until it survived 100 days, as such a relationship lasting 100 days requires a celebration (and you better keep count, guys!).
- 발렌타인데이 [bal-len-ta-in da-e] Valentine's Day
  In Korea, women prepare chocolate for men on Feb. 14th.
  The men respond the following month by giving candy
  on Mar. 14th, which is called White Day (화이트데이), .
- 블랙데이 [beul-lack-da-i] Black Day – for those sad souls who have no boyfriend or girlfriend, April 14th brings Black Day. Celebrated alone or with friends by eating black noodles called *jjajangmyeon* (자장면).
- 투투데이 [tu-tu-dae-i] 22 days dating (like 100 days, but less common)

출퇴

[chul-tui]

to sneak out; take roll and run

문자 그대로 '출석하고 나서 튄다'는 말로, 줄임말인 출퇴가 친구들 사이에서 수업을 빠지고 놀자고 부르는 말로 흔해지게 되었다. 이 표현은 고등학교 때 학업의 의무를 다하고 지금이 놀아야할 때라고 느끼는 대학생들 사이에서 주로 사용된다. 또한 이 표현은 국회 본회의에 출석하지 않은 국회의원들을 가리켜 쓰기도 한다! (아 이런!)

Literally "to take attendance and bounce" from *chulseokhago naseo tuida* 출석하고 나서 튄다), the abbreviated version of *chultui* became common as a call between friends to skip out and go play. This expression, though primarily used for university students who have paid their dues in the study hell of high school and feel that now is their only time to play, is also used for National Assembly members who skip out on plenary sessions! (Oh my!)

Also: 먹퇴 [meok-tui] to dine and dash, or to skip out on a obligation (e.g. a sports player making a contract then skipping out)

야간수업

KwangSung 너무 좋지? 수업 빠지고 술 마시러 가기로 결정한 거.

ByungShik 응. 출퇴는 계속 칠판만 쳐다보고 있는 김교수님한테 항상 먹히지.

KwangSung 근데 화석이는 어딨어? 걔도 출퇴같이 하기로 했잖아.

ByungShik 무슨 상관이야! 술이나 마시자…

〔한참 후〕

HwaSeok 얘들아! 너네 어디 갔었어?

ByungShik 우리 출퇴했지! 너는?

HwaSeok 오, 출퇴하기 나쁜 날 골랐구나! 쉬는시간에 교수님이 우리 데리고 갈비랑 술 쏘셨는데.

KwangSung 헐!

Night Class

광성	Isn't this great? So glad we decided to skip class and go drinking?
병식	Yeah, chultui always works with Prof. Kim. staring at the board all the time.
광성	But where's HwaSeok? He was supposed to chultui too.
병식	Who cares! Let's drink...

[much later]

화석	Hey guys! Where did you go?
병식	We did chultui! Why didn't you?
화석	Oh, You picked a bad day for chultui! At the break, the professor decided to take us all out for kalbi and drinks.
광성	Heol!

University Section

From High School Hell to the College Liberation Jam

College is a special time for Korean students, finally out of the pressure hell of high school, they start to let loose and feel liberated, freeing themselves of authority figures, hellish study schedules and restrictions (alcohol, etc.).

• **긱사긱사** [gag-sa gig-sa] dorm (onomatopoeia)

• **과잠** [gua-jang] department major uniform (letter jacket)

• **출튀 (출석하고 튄다)** [chul-tui (chul-seok-ha-go tuin-da)] to be in class for attendance and then leave (sneak out)

• **대출** [dae-chul] short for **대리출석** [dae-ri chul-seok] meaning to take attendance for someone else. A great example of which is in the movie: "Sassy Girl" – **엽기적인그녀 (영화)**.

• **공강** [gong-gang] free period between classes

• **학식 (학교식당음식)** [hak-shik (hak-kyo-shik-dang-eum-shik)] school cafeteria food. So gross!

• **주사파** [ju-sa-pa] schedule class only 4 days a week (also **주삼파** or **주오파**)

Mockingly Clear and Cold

Absolute in its aspiration,
kiok's ⌐ keen mind crippled with ambition.

        Crazily k'ed in a crucial moment...

The big brother of ⌐ began in jest to foment

  with somewhat of a snigger, then bellied and bold

      began to chuckle, mockingly clear and cold,

Kh kh kh ⌐ ⌐ ⌐, as K's insanity took hold.

컨닝하다

[cun-ning-ha-da]

to cheat on tests; to be cunning

한국에서 "컨닝"은 영어 의미와 별개의 의미를 갖는다. 콩글리쉬화 된 이 단어의 뜻은 시험에서 베끼는 것을 의미한다(몇몇의 한국인들은 아주 어려운 시험에 있어서 베끼는 것은 가끔은 해도 되는 것이라고 얘기한다).

"Cunning" in Korea is largely independent of the English meaning. The Konglicized version is to "cheat on a test (and get away with it)" with the connotation of "… like a fox," and often said with pride as some young Koreans think that cheating is an acceptable way of overcoming the impossible expectations of the school system).

시험점수

ByungShik	얘들아, SAT점수 나왔대… 보러가자!
KwangSung	야! 나는 640점, 화석이는 660점이야.
ByungShik	수학 아니면 언어? 난 수학은 겨우 600, 언어는 540인데.
KwangSung	아니 합쳐서.
ByungShik	뭐? 난 너 컨닝한줄 알았는데?
KwangSung	나 화석이꺼 컨닝했어. 그리고 걔는 내꺼 컨닝하고.
ByungShik	바보냐! 다음에는 좀 똑똑한 애 옆에 앉아라!!

Test Scores

병식	Guys, the SAT scores are posted … Let's go see?
광성	Hey! I got a 640 and HwaSeok got a 660.
병식	On math or verbal? I only got 600 math and 540 verbal.
광성	No, combined.
병식	What? I thought you did cunning?
광성	I did cunning off HwaSeok. And he did cunning off of me.
병식	You idiots! You're supposed to sit next to someone smart!!

Tried and True, Tiut Withdrew

from the public life it once knew.
An extra line across digut ꞇ cut
to tell that it was tough enough for what
was to come. . . . Aspirated fully.
Separate and gruff, but no bully.
Voiced and vocal tiut ꞇ grew
strong and bold, though somewhat askew.
" ꞇ, ꞇ, ꞇ," it tutted trailing, uttering slowly it s last "adieu."

태클걸다

[tae-keul-geol-da]

to cock-block; to butt in

이 콩글리쉬 표현은 '누군가에게 태클하는 것'을 의미하는 영어로부터 유래하였다. 그러나 한국인들은 이것을 비속어로써 이성에게 작업하는 것을 방해할 때, 혹은 누군가 무엇을 하려 하는 것을 방해할 때 사용하고 있다. 이는 이성 앞에서 상대방을 깎아내려 자신을 중요하게 보이려는 경우 등 친구들 사이에서 주로 쓰인다.

This Konglish expression comes from the English for tackling someone. However the Koreans use it as slang for cock-blocking, picking a fight, or to provoke a quarrel with someone in order to disrupt whatever they are trying to do. It is often used between friends to cut someone down in front of the opposite sex when they are trying to look important, etc.

번외 게임

ChangHyun	야 임마, 나한테 태클걸지마!
SiWoo	태클도 게임의 일부야. 이게 축구고 넌 너무 느려.
ChangHyun	저기 있는 내 새 여자친구랑 걔 친구들한테 잘 보이려고 하고있잖아… 숏 좀 하게 해주라.
SiWoo	알았다, 알았어, 그럼 새끼 좀 쳐주고 내가 꼬실때 태클걸지마.

The Side Game

창현	Hey man, don't taekeulgeolda me!
시우	Tackling is part of the game. It's soccer and you are too slow.
창현	I'm trying to look good for my new girl and her friend over there … let me at least take a shot.
시우	All right, all right, but introduce me to her friend and don't taekeulgeolda me when I try to pick her up.

토끼다

[to-ggi-da]

to skip out; dine and dash

글자 그대로, "이거 토끼야." 이것은 무언가를 먹고 지불하지 않은 채 도망가는 것, 혹은 무언가를 훔쳐 달아나는것을 의미한다. 이와 비슷한 영어식 표현으로는 "Dine and dash."가 있다. 영화 Cool Hand Luke에서의 "gets a rabbit in him"을 떠오르게 한다. 유의어 – 튀다와 째다가 있다. (또한 수업, 야자를 하지 않고 도망 갈 때도 쓸 수 있다.)

Literally "it's a rabbit." This means to eat something and run away (not paying the bill) or to steal something and hightail it out of there. Similar to the English expression "Dine and dash," and calls to mind the scene from Cool Hand Luke, when his mama dies and he "gets a rabbit in him." (Can also mean to skip class or study hall.)

Synonyms: 튀다 [tui-da] to bounce, bound; 째다 [jjae-da] to rip or cleave; cut out (on a bill); 먹튀[meok-tui] to dine and dash.

병식이 레스토랑

MyongTae	나 돈 없어… 토끼는거 어때?
SaengTae	좋은 생각이야, 여기서 먹고 싶은 거 다 먹고 그냥 튀면 돼.
MyongTae	그래, 그럼 쨀까?
ByungShik	얘들아, 나 다 들었거든. 토끼려고 하기 전에 내가 군 제대 얼마 전에 해서, 토끼보다 빠른걸 기억해라. 그리고 도망가면 쫓아가서 인도에서 튀어나가 두 놈을 다 째지게 하겠어.

ByungShik's Restaurant

명태	I'm short of cash … what do you say we toggida?
생태	Great idea, we can just tuida up out of here after we eat all we want!
명태	OK, let's jjaeda?
병식	Hey guys, I heard everything, so before you try a toggida, just remember that I finished army service, so I'm faster than a rabbit, and I'll bounce you off the sidewalk and rip you in two.

토나오다

[to-na-o-da]

make me puke; hell no

글자 그대로, "토할 것 같다." 어떠한 제안이나 아이디어에 반감을 갖고 있어 "소화기관"
에서 게워 낼 정도로 싫음의 의미를 내포하고 있다. 비슷한 영어 표현으로는 "Hell no!"
혹은 "You've got to be kidding."가 있다.

Literally "I'm going to throw up." The Korean implies a disgust with some suggestion
or idea, providing a physical or "gut" response that is as hateful as vomiting. Similar
to the English "Hell no!" "You've got to be kidding!" or "Don't make me puke!"

쥐꼬리 책 2

Peter	시우야, 이 책 끝나는대로, 다른 책 또 쓰자.
SiWoo	토나온다. 토나와.
Peter	뭐? 너 어디 아파?
SiWoo	아니, 나 미치게 하고 싶냐고!

Rat's Tail Book 2

피터	Hey SiWoo, as soon as we finish this book, let's write another one.
시우	Tonaoda. Tonawa.
피터	What? Are you going to be sick?
시우	No, are you trying to make me crazy?!

Puke Box

A Gag, a Yearning, a Slow Stomach Turning...

- **구토** [gu-to] to vomit (spew, heave, wretch, puke, purge, hurl or barf).
- **오바이트** [o-bai-teu] throw up, taking it's sound from the English "over-eat"
- **토** [to] vomit (short form).
- **휔** [huaek] or **우웩** [uwaek] onomatopoeia for throwing up or "losing one's lunch." --Keep it down, fellas!

튕기다

[twing-gi-da]

to act coy or feign refusal (and then concede)

글자 그대로는 '끈을 뜯다 당기다, 혹은 악기의 줄을 튕기는 것'을 의미하는 말. 실제의 뜻은 사랑의 기교, 혹은 설득력과 관계가 있다. 한 남자가 여자의 손목을 잡으려고 애쓰고, 그녀도 원하기는 하지만 수줍어하는 척하며 여성적으로 보여 거부하는 모습을 떠올릴 수 있다.

Literally "to pluck strings" or "twang an instrument." The actual meaning is a type of skill in the art of love or persuasion. Imagine a man trying to grab his woman's wrist and she plucks it away in feigned act of bashful femininity, yet wants him to grab it again.

보상없는 사랑 2

DongWon   원동아 아까 희연이였어? 왜 그냥 걸어가버려?

WonDong   걔는 항상 나 가지고 놀잖아... 끊임없이 튕긴다.

DongWon   아, 사랑의 음악...

WonDong   사랑? 하도 오랫동안 줄을 튕겨대서 더 이상의 튕은 없다. 포기했어!

DongWon   니 말은 방금 깨진거라고?

WonDong   사실 시작한적도 없지, 걔가 튕긴것 밖에는.

Unrequited Love 2

동원   WonDong, was that HeeYeon? Why is she walking away?

원동   Yeah, she's always playing with me ...
Continually twinggida.

동원   Ah, the music of love ...

원동   Love? She's been pulling my strings so long that there's no twing left. I give up!

동원   You mean you just broke up?

원동   Actually, we never got started, she just did twinggida.

216

The Power of Piup

The perfect, playful piup ㅍ said:

    I might spit a bit, but I've shed

        all pretense for a life of pleasure,

    As the aspiration of all aspirates treasure

        Not a wimp like that babbling biup ㅂ

Piup ㅍ put it to all with proper measure of power.

    Its purpose passion voiced, its eyes moist

      as some characters cowered . . . and some rejoiced.

88만원 세대

[88man-won sae-dae]

the $880 generation

2007년, 한 경제학자가 20대 대학 졸업생의 5%만이 성공적인 직장을 갖고 나머지 95%
는 평균 월급 88만원의 비정규직으로 남게 될 것이라고 예상한 〈88만원 세대〉라는 책을
썼다. 이로부터 88만원 세대라는 용어가 만들어 졌으며 그 이후 현재의 치열한 취업 시장
에서 많은 사람들에게 냉혹한 현실이 되었다.

In 2007, an economist wrote a book called "The $880 Generation" predicting that
only 5% of people in their 20's who graduate college will find successful jobs, and
the remaining 95% will be stuck in temp jobs that only earn an average of $880
dollars a month. Thus the *880manwon saedae* was coined and has come to be a
grim reality for many in the current challenging job market.

관점

HeeYeon	88만원 세대의 한 사람이라는 건 정말 힘들지 않니? 정말 오랫동안 구직만 하고 있잖아. 이제는 정말 편의점에서 일해야 할까봐.
MinJi	멋지다. 너 영화 Clerks 봤니?
HeeYeon	응, 근데 그건 그냥 20대의 고뇌와 미래가 없는 직업의 구렁텅이에 관한 거잖아. 난 고대 출신이야. 대기업의 꿈을 이루고 싶다구!
MinJi	나한테 필요한 건 남자친구랑, 그리고…; 내 용돈 뿐이야.
HeeYeon	넌 이태백이 되는게 불안하지도 않니? 88만원 세대가 우릴 망치고 말거야.
MinJi	나는 백수인 게 좋은데. 88만원? ㅋㅋ 난 매달 화장품에만 그만큼씩 쓰는데.

Perspectives

희연   It's so difficult to be part of this 88man-won saedae? I've been looking for a job for ages. Now I'm going to have to work at a convenience store.

민지   How cool. Did you see the movie Clerks?

희연   Yeah, but that's all about 20-something angst and the purgatory of a dead end job. I studied at Kodae! I want the corporate dream!

민지   All I need is a boyfriend…; and my allowance.

희연   Aren't you worried about becoming an i-tae-baek? This 88man-won saedae is going to ruin us.

민지   I love being a baeksu. $880? Kh, kh. I spend that much on my makeup every month.

퍼뜩

[peo-ddeuk]

a sudden flash of inspiration

이것은 다소 의성어 혹은 의태어적인 표현이다. 고기가 물 밖으로 나와 퍼덕거리는 것과 같이 무언가 갑자기 잃어난 것을 의미한다. 특별히 영감이나 아이디어가 물방울과 같이 갑자기 떠올랐을 때 쓰인다. 유의어 - 후딱

This is a somewhat onomatopoeic or mimetic expression for something happening suddenly, like a fish out of water, flapping around. It is most often used for a sudden flash of inspiration or an idea striking one's mind like a drop of water.

Synonym: 후딱 [hu-ddak] quickly or nimbly; as quick as a thought.

배트맨의 최악의 아이디어!

Robin	우리 조커를 어떻게 해야되지, 배트맨?
Batman	음, 생각 좀 해보자… 아, 퍼뜩! 생각났다.
Robin	뭐? 중국의 물고문? 물벌?
Batman	아니, 우리가 조크를 하면 걘 조커니까 조크 마무리 하러 올거고, 그럼 그때 후딱! 잡으면 돼.

Holy Bad Idea, Batman!

로빈	What can we do about the Joker, Batman?
배트맨	Hmmm, let me think … Ah, peoddeuk! I have an idea.
로빈	What? Chinese water torture? Water boarding?
배트맨	No, we'll start a joke and he'll have to come finish it, and then huddak! We'll grab him.

폭탄이다

[pok-tan-i-da]

butt-ugly or busted

간단히 말해, 폭탄은 bomb이다. 비속어로 외모가 심각하게 못생겨 아무도 데이트하고 싶어하지 않음을 나타내는 표현이다. 비슷한 영어표현으로는 "it sucks." 또는 경멸하는 의미의 "busted"가 있다.

Simply speaking, *poktan* is a bomb. As slang, this expression refers to a person's definitive unattractiveness, or someone that no one wants to end up with. Opposite of the English expression "the bomb," it is used to describe someone as hideous, revolting or more appropriately with the derogatory term "busted."

잃어버린 번역 2

Peter	제시카 알바는 폭탄이다!
Siwoo	너 정신 나갔어? 걔 완전 예뻐…
Peter	그래 당연하지. 걔는 똥이야!
Siwoo	똥이라니 무슨말이야. 나 걔 사랑해… 저번에 니가 소개시켜준 여자가 폭탄이다! 그래서 내가 튄거야.
Peter	알았다, 알았어. 내 생각에 우린 비속어 번역가가 필요할 것 같아. 니가 센스없는 소리만 계속 하잖아.
Siwoo	잘못 짚었어. 그건 너지. 하지만 그래, 그 쥐꼬리 책에서 한번 찾아보자.

Lost in Translation 2

피터	Jessica Alba is poktanida! She's the bomb!
시우	Are you insane? She's beautiful!…
피터	Yeah, man. She's the shit!
시우	What do you mean shit. I love her… The girl you introduced me to was poktanida! That's why I bounced.
피터	OK, I guess we need a slang translator, cause you're not making any sense.
시우	You've got it the wrong way, but yeah, let's look at that "Rat's Tail" book again.

품절(남/녀)

[pum-jeol(nam/yeo)]

(someone) taken; sold out; unavailable

문자 그대로 품절된 사람을 가리키는 이 표현은 결혼하여 상대가 될 수 없는 (특히 대어라 고 여겨질 만 한) 사람을 의미하게 되었다. 영어의 "off the market" 혹은 "taken"과 비 슷하다.

Literally meaning someone who is "sold-out" or "out of stock." This expression has come to mean someone (especially someone that would be considered quite a catch) that is married off and otherwise no longer available. Similar to "off the market" or "taken" in English.

Also: 반품(남,녀) [ban-pum-(nam/yeo)] back on the market, lit. to return (a product).

올드보이 2

HaPum	세상에. 너 그 소식 들었니?
HanSum	무슨 소식?
HaPum	지태가 드디어 결혼했대… 민식의 딸이랑. 역시.
HanSum	아, 또 다른 품절남. 너무 슬프다.
HaPum	품절이라고? 농담하지 마!
HanSum	매우 큰 손해야. 아까워! 난 그냥 그가 반품남이 되길 바라며 기다려야겠다.
HaPum	너 미쳤구나!

Old boy 2

하품	Oh, my. Did you see the news?
한숨	What news?
하품	JiTae finally got married… And to MinShik's daughter no less.
한숨	Oh, another pumjoelnam. So sad.
하품	Pumjeol?! You must be kidding!
한숨	Such a loss. So regrettable! I'll just have to wait and hope for him to become banpumnam.
하품	You're sick!

피봤어

[pi-boass-eo]

it sucked; what a bummer

글자 그대로, 자신의 피를 보다. 이 관용어는 어떠한 좋지 않은 사건, 상황으로부터 손해를 입음을 나타낸다. 느낌상, 이는 나에게 타격을 준 아주 나쁜 것.

Literally "I saw my blood." This idiom refers to the damage one received from some unpleasant circumstance, in a sense, it sucked so bad that it damaged me. Related to the English expression "bummer man."

끝내주는 직업정신?

DooHwan	어이, 박통. 연설 어땠어?
ChungHee	오, 피봤어! 피봤어! 내 손에 피…
DooHwan	왜, 잘 안됐어? 연설 망쳐버린거야?
ChungHee	아니, 누군가 나를 쏘려하다가 실패했고, 걔 잡았어!
DooHwan	그래 그럼 괜찮은거네, 근데 연설은 중지됐겠다. 그지?
ChungHee	아니, 연설 끝까지 다 했어. 오, 피봤어!
DooHwan	그럼 피본건 뭔데?
ChungHee	걔들이 내 아내 죽였거든! 피가 사방에 튀고. 피봤어!

A True Professional?

두환	Hey, President Park. How was the speech?
정희	Oh, piboasseo! Piboasseo! Blood on my hands …
두환	What, it was terrible? You messed up the speech?
정희	No, someone tried to shoot me, but he missed and we caught him!
두환	So you're OK, but you had to stop the speech, right?
정희	No, I finished the speech. Oh, piboasseo!
두환	Then what was piboasseo?
정희	They killed my wife! There was blood everywhere. piboasseo!

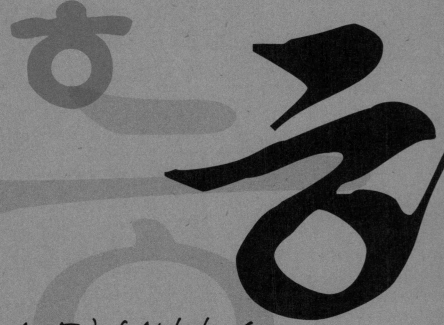

An End of Alphabet Comes

Humming happily to a hiut ㅎ breeze,
somewhat soft with a bit of a wheeze.
Devoid of drums, the delicate hum
is aspirated in a breath of cold air ease.
Hiut covers the gamut from hair to fair,
From ha ha 하하 happy to the ㅎㅎ sarcastic glare.
And forget "Fighting," cause in Korean it's "Highting!"
There's no F after all, so "Hip, hip, hiut" for all.

허접

[heo-jeob]

you suck (at an online game)

초라한, 보잘것 없는 것을 뜻하는 허섭쓰레기라는 단어로부터 유래되었다. 이는 허접쓰레기로 변형되었다가 다시 허접이라는 말로 줄여져 '무언가 잘하지 못하는 것, 혹은 아주 형편없음을 의미'한다. 주로 스타크래프트와 같은 온라인게임에서 사용된다.

Taken from the word *heoseob-seuraegi* (허섭쓰레기) meaning a shabby, humble, or worn-out thing, it was distorted to *heojeob-seuraegi* (허접쓰레기) and then shortened to *heojeob*. The slang meaning is to be lousy at something or to suck, and it is most often used in reference to online gaming such as StarCraft.

모욕주기

Peter	창현아, 스타크래프트 한판 할까?
ChangHyun	장난하냐? 넌 허접이야.
Peter	무슨 소리 하는거야? 나 스타크래프트 할 줄 알아...
ChangHyun	그래, 근데 너 전화벨만 울리면 도망가잖아.
Peter	그건, 사업상 전화가 올 때...
ChangHyun	사업? 여자 꼬시는 사업이겠지! 너는 여자한테만 말 걸잖아!!
Peter	적어도 난 그런 일이라도 있지...
	너야말로 데이트 허접인거야.

Trash Talk

피터	Hey ChangHyun, you wanna play StarCraft?
창현	Are you kidding? You're heojjeob.
피터	What? I can play StarCraft...
창현	Yeah, but you always walk away when your phone rings.
피터	Well, that's if it's business...
창현	Business? The business of picking up girls!
	You only talk to girls!!
피터	At least I have game...
	Maybe that's why you are so heojeob at dating.

하의실종

[ha-eui-shil-jong]

scantily clad; MIA bottoms

문자 그대로 사라진 하의, 즉 사라진 치마나 바지를 말한다. 어떤 사람의 다리가 거의 덮여 있지 않아 거의 하의를 입고있지 않은 것처럼 보이거나 하의가 실종된 것처럼 보일 때 쓴다.

Literally "a disappearing bottom, skirt or shorts." When someone's lower half or *ha* is so scantily covered that it seems as if they are naked on the bottom or their clothing (*eui*) is missing in action (*shiljong*).

과거의 망령

GeunHye	그만! 이놈의 하의실종 치마랑 핫팬츠 더이상 못참겠다!
Psy	내가 제일 좋아하는 것들인데!
GeunHye	그건 과다노출일 뿐이야! 젊은 여성들한테 부적절해! 새로운 법을 만들어야겠어!
Psy	그치만 네 이 오래된 해변가 사진은 뭔데?
GeunHye	어, 음…
Psy	그 비키니는 진짜 하의실종인걸!
GeunHye	어, 글쎄. 그건 그 때고…
Psy	스스로를 감추지 마, 씨스타! 그리고 부디 서울의 매끈한 다리의 즐거움을 뺏지 말아줘.

A Haunting Past

근혜	That's it! I've had it with these haeuishiljong skirts and short shorts.
싸이	Those are my favorite!
근혜	It's simply over-exposure! Not appropriate for young ladies! I'm going to make a new law!
싸이	What about this old picture of you at the beach?
근혜	Uh, um…
싸이	That bikini is seriously haeuishiljong!
근혜	Uh, well. That was then…
싸이	Keep it real, sister! And don't take away the leggy joy of Seoul.

Culturally Speaking

The 'Height' of Fashion

Modesty in women's attire in Korea, tends to be limited to the upper half as showing legs up to the crotch is commonplace. Short shorts and even shorter skirts are aplenty, yet showing even the slightest bit of cleavage is a major no-no in the exceptionally conservative Land of the Morning Calm. Korea, however, seems to be somewhat selective about this conservative nature with a dichotomy that spans the ubiquitousness of love motels (with parking lot curtains to protect the innocent, of course) to the feigned innocence of unmarried women (Or is it real? Who knows…) and the neon crosses of Christian zealotry dotting the landscape.

Somehow the legs have gotten a pass and with some serious *haeuishiljong* and *gulbokji* going around, who's to complain? Not I for one!

헐

[heol]

OMG; oops; tisk; huh?; whatever; what can I say...

상당히 다이내믹하면서도 여전히 다소 모호한 의미로, 누군가 다른 사람의 말에 놀라거나 당황했을 때 간단히 "헐"로 대답할 수 있다. 조금은 빈정대는 투로서의 "Oh my God"과 약간의 "huh?!"의 의미까지 섞여 있는 듯하다. 이는 단순히 있을 수 없는 일에 대한 가벼운 충격, 놀람, 혹은 실망의 표현이다. 이것은 또한 메시지 상에서 강조하기 위해 헐ㅜㅜ 로 사용될 수 있으며, 누군가 귀여워 보이려 할 때(보통 여자)는 헐랭이나 헐퀴로도 쓰일 수 있다.

Rather dynamic and still somewhat vague in meaning, one would simply respond with "*heol*" when surprised or even embarrassed by another's statement. Somewhat similar to "oh my God" with a bit of sarcasm and even a little "huh?!" in the mix. *Heol* an expression of mild shock, surprise, or disappointment about something that simply doesn't make sense (doesn't compute). It can also be appended with 헐ㅜㅜ for added emphasis when texting, or 헐랭 [*heol-rang*] or even 헐퀴 [*heol-kui*] for someone trying to be cute (usually a girl).

헐보이

HaPum	그래서 민식은 지태가 자기 누나한테 키스하는 것을 보게 돼.
HanSum	헐. 〔그거 역겹다!〕
HaPum	그리고 지태는 민식을 납치하고, 아무런 설명도 없이 15년 동안이나 방에 감금하고는 줄곧 민식이 그의 딸을 사랑하게 만들어.
HanSum	헐. 〔왜 그렇게 해?!〕
HaPum	그런데 전체 내용은 그저 오이디푸스 신화를 고쳐 쓴 것 같아.
HanSum	헐. 〔완전 나쁘다.〕

HeolBoy

하품	So MinShik sees JiTae kissing his sister.
한숨	Heol. [that's gross!]
하품	Then JiTae kidnapped MinShik and imprisoned him in a room for 15 years without explanation, all the while making him fall in love with his own daughter.
한숨	Heol. [but why?!]
하품	But the whole story is just the story of Oedipus retold.
한숨	Heol. [too bad.]

환장하다

[huan-jang-ha-da]

to go mad for; to be crazy about

글자 그대로 해석하면, 장이 꼬이는 것 바꿈을 의미하는 환(換)과 장을 의미하는 장(腸)의 한자로부터 유래하였다. 실제의 뜻은 미칠 지경인 것, 그러나 이는 또한 무언가에 완전히 미쳐있어 종종 어떤것에 대해 마음이 완전히 바뀌어있음을 나타내기도 한다.

Literally "overthrowing intestines," from the Chinese character *huan* (換) meaning to overthrow and *jang* (腸) meaning intestines. The actual meaning is "to go mad or go out of one's mind," but it is also often used to describe someone who has gone mad for something that involves a complete change of heart.

곱창에 대한 잡담

MinHee	뭐 먹을까?
HeeYeon	곱창 어때?
MinHee	너 미친거야? 환장했네? 너 곱창 싫어하잖아!
HeeYeon	그랬지, 하지만 지금은 곱창에 환장해. 어서 가자!
MinHee	너 완전히 환장했구나! 난 아직도 곱창이 싫다규 – 징그러워!

Chatting about Chitterlings

민희	What should we eat?
희연	How about geopchang?
민희	Have you gone mad? Did you huanjanghada?
	You hate geopchang!
희연	I did, but now I'm huanjanghada for them. Let's go!
민희	You're completely huanjanghada!
	And you know I still hate them – Gross!

The Straight Scoop

곱창 [geob-chang] the Korean equivalent to chitterlings or cows intestines. Yum!

229

후까시 잡다

[hu-gga-shi jab-da]

sudden pretense

후까시는 일본말로서 '눈으로 볼 수 없음을 의미'한다. 여기서 이는 어떤 겉치레하는 것을 의미하여, 특별히 위엄있는 척을 할 경우 사용된다.

Huggashi [후가시] is the Japanese word for invisibility (or as a verb, to show off), and *japta* [잡다] is Korean for to seize or grab. In essence, it means to grab at the unattainable or putting on some pretense, particularly pretending to be dignified when one normally is anything but. Similar to the English expression "cop an attitude," in particular, for an overly competitive person, or even someone who coifs their hair high or wears risers in their shoes to make themselves look taller.

점잔빼는 말

ChangHyun   (통화중) 예, 알겠습니다. 감사합니다... 아닙니다. 확실히 하겠습니다.

Peter   뭐하는거야? 너 존댓말 절대 안쓰잖아.

     누구때문에 후까시 잡는건데?

ChangHyun   직장 상사랑 전화하느라고 그런거야. 근데 니가 어떻게 아냐?

     너 존댓말 한 글자도 모르잖아.

Peter   알지 왜몰라... 후까시 잡기 싫어서 그러는것 뿐이지.

     난 편안하게 대화하고 싶다고. 난 격식따위에 신경쓰지 않으니까.

ChangHyun   물론 그러시겠죠. 머리에 똥만 차가지고!

Proper Fucking Language

창현   (on phone) Ah, Yes sir, thank you sir… No, sir.
Yes, I certainly will, sir.

피터   What? You never use polite language. For whom is this huggashi jabda?

창현   Just talking to my superior officer. And how do you know?
You don't even know any formal language.

피터   Of course I do… I just don't like to huggashi jabda.
I like to speak comfortably. I'm full of informality.

창현   You're full of something all right!

Culturally Speaking

Sir, Yes Sir!

Languages are defined by culture; this is particularly true for Korean as Honorifics in the language are dictated by the situation or relationship of the people communicating. With different words and structures used for people that are older or more senior in some position or for public speaking (높은말 [nop-in-mal] high-formal language), peers of the same age or same level in the work environment (존댓말 [jon-daet-mal] polite informal), and those of lower age or position (반말 [ban-mal] informal).

Many non-native speakers find it difficult to understand or at least get used the sometimes complicated language, particularly of the marked differences of language of a news program vs. the conversations one has with peers. Additionally, the rapid changes necessary in a conversation of mixed levels. Finally, *banmal* can be used with someone that should be spoken to with formal or polite language to deliberately insult them. (This too often happens to foreigners in Korea who might not catch the insult.)

흑역사

[heuk-yeok-sa]

dark history; embarrassing past

역사는 종종 되돌아와 우리를 괴롭힐 때가 있다. 우리가 겪어 온 잘못된 헤어스타일 선택에서부터 창피한 고스시절까지, 우리의 어두운 역사는 가끔씩 현재에 그 모습을 드러내기도 한다. 흑역사는 문자 그대로 검은 역사를 의미하지만 원래는 과거의 전쟁이나 역사상 암울한 시절을 가리켰다. '현재는 차라리 잊어버리고 싶은 그러한 과거의 시절들을 의미' 하게 되었다.

History often comes back to haunt us. From our poor choices in hairstyles to the embarrassing Goth phase we went through in high school, our dark history sometimes finds its way to the light of the present day. *Heukyeoksa* is literally 'black history' and though it originally referred to past wars or other dark periods in history, it has come to denote those times in our past that we'd rather forget.

과거의 망령 2

GeunHye   음, 너도 분명 과거의 비밀이 있을 거야. 흑역사 말야.

(동갑)   아냐, 아냐, 아니야! 난 언제나 완벽했다구. 헤헤.

GeunHye   너의 그 이중고는 어쩌고? 네가 군대를 두 번 복무했다고
들었는데 말야.

Psy   맞아, 그치만 모든 사람들이 다 아는 일인걸.

GeunHye   오, 그리고 대마초! 너 진짜 나쁜 애구나! 감옥도 다녀오고.

Psy   난 사실 꽤 자랑스러워… 나에게 길거리 명성을 줬거든.

GeunHye   그럼 뭐? 분명 흑역사가 있을 거 아냐.. 어떤 창피한 과거 말야.

Psy   나한테 흑역사는 그 지퍼달린 나일론 낙하산 바지 브레이크 댄스야.

GeunHye   오, 그건 진짜 창피하다.

A Haunting Past 2

근혜	Well, you must have some secrets from your past, some heukyeoksa too.
싸이	No, no, no! I've always been perfect. He he.
근혜	What about the double trouble? I heard you had to serve in the army twice.
싸이	Sure, but everybody knows that.
근혜	Oh, and the pot! You were a very bad boy! You did some jail time, I see.
싸이	I'm kinda proud of that... it gives me street cred.
근혜	Then what? There must be some heukyeoksa... some shameful past.
싸이	For me, that heukyeoksa was the zippered nylon parachute pants breakdancing thing.
근혜	Oh, that is bad.

Appendix

Swear Box

Be careful!! Shhh! Don't say these, but you should know what they mean... especially if you are watching gangster movies... Korean Swearing in brief:

The Basics

- 년 [nyeon] bitch
- 놈 [nom] bastard
- 좆 [jot] dick or cock
- 개 [gae] dog or cur (used with other swears to suggest SOB)
- 개새끼 [gae-sae-ggi] SOB – son of a bitch (literally "a dog's offspring") can also be shortened to 개새 [gae-sae]. A student once talked of a beautiful English expression – Sun of a Beach – oops!
- 씨발 [ssi-bal] similar to "you fucking (so-and-so)" in English, but literally meaning "you will sell your seed." This can be shortened to 씹 [sshib]
- 쌍 [ssang] low-born or ignoble from Chosun dynasty or before, also 쌍 [sshyang] most often used as a combination 쌍놈 [ssang-nom] low bastard
- 미친 [mi-chin] crazy, most often used as a combination 미친새끼 [mi-chin sae-ggi] crazy SOB, 미친년 [mi-chin nyeon] crazy bitch, or 미친놈 [mi-chin nom] crazy bastard
- ㅗㅗ [o-o] texting for "fuck you," as it resembles two middle fingers sticking up.

Sex Box

The Acts

- 섹스 [sek-se] sex (borrowed from English, ubiquitous)
- 하다 [ha-da] to do it (have sex)
- 자다 [ja-da] to sleep with (sex)
- 합궁 [hap-geung] having sex (archaic, a bit like "making house")
- 성교 [seong-gyo] intercourse (coitus or sexual congress)
- 몸을 섞다 [moem-eul seogg-da] to mix bodies (have sexual intercourse)
- 성관계 [seong-gwan-gae] to have sexual relations (more of a medical term)
- 혼전성관계 [hon-jeon seong-gwan-gae] to have premarital sex
- (성욕을) 자극하다 [seong-yuk-eul ja-geug-ha-da] - arouse sexual desire
- 딸딸이 [ddal-ddal-i] masterbating (childish) - for a bit of fun on your own
- 자위하다 [ja-ui-ha-da] beat off or jack off
- 수음을 하다 [su-eom-eul ha-da] to play with oneself (also a hand job)
- 구강 성교 [gu-gang seong-gyo] fellatio or cunnilingus
- 사까시 [sa-gga-si] oral sex (from the Japanese)
- 빠구리 [bba-gu-rl] buggery (doggy-style ass fucking)
- 섹스숍 [sek-se-shop] or 포르노점(店) [po-re-no-jeom] - a place to buy those awesome toys or little nightin-nothings
- 야설 [ya-seol] an erotic novel, an acronym of 야한 소설 [ya-han so-seol]

Some Other Stuff

- 걸레 [geol-lae] a slut or easy woman who will sleep with anyone (lit. a rag)
- 갈보 [gal-bo] or 창녀 [chang-yeo] a prostitute, a whore. (North Korea recently called South Korean President Park GeunHye a crafty whore (교활한 창녀 [kyo-hwal-han chang-yeo]). BAD form boys!
- 싸보이다 [ssa-bo-i-da] looks cheap (like a prostitute)
- 떡뷁이 [ddeok-bogg-i] magic sex (during the woman's period)
- 라뷁이 [ra-bogg-i] magic pubes (red pubic hair that results from having sex during the woman's period)

The Body Parts – the unmentionables

The Organs of Love

- 보지 [bo-ji] muff, cunt or pussy (slang for a vulva and related to a flower), also 뽕 [bbong] or 잠지 [jam-ji]
- 자지 [ja-ji] penis (offensive, similar to the English dick or cock) also 좆 [jot]
- 좆나게 [jot-na-gae] to get hard (for the penis to come out)
- 고추 [go-chu] literally "a pepper," but childish slang for a penis as with pee-pee or wee-wee.
- 물건 [mul-geon] literally, a thing (slang for the penis) like "down there" or "it"
- 젖 [jeot] breast or breast milk, also 젖가슴 [jeot-ga-seum] boobs or tits
- 젖탱이 [jeot-taeng-i] the cup of the breasts, 찌찌 [jji-jji] breast (childish)
- 유두 [yu-du] nipples or 젖꼭지 [jeot-ggok-ji] literally, the breast spigot

Other (questionably innocent) Body Parts

The Butt – in Korea, words related to the butt, anus or feces are not nearly as taboo as they are in English, so they are not generally considered swear words or even foul language, but would still not be used in polite conversation.

- 엉덩이 [eong-deong-i], 엉댕이 [eong-daeng-i], 궁둥이 [gong-deung-i], 궁댕이 [gong-daeng-i] and 히프 [hip] all mean butt, but do not equate with "ass."
- 항문 [hang-mun] anus (medical term)
- 똥구멍 [ddong-gu-meong], 뚱구녕 [ddeong-gu-nyeong] and 똥꼬 [ddeong-go] all mean poop-hole, but do not carry the same weight as "asshole" in English.

A Bad Hair Day – We've all had one, but these are far from what you're thinking!

- 좆털 [jot-teol] a man's pubic hair (literally "cock fur")
- 잡털 [jab-teol] a man's pubic hair (literally "impure fur")
- 보지털 [bo-ji-tol] a woman's pubic hair (literally "pussy fur")

Mouth, Ears and Eyes – Koreans expect others to keep their secrets without asking, putting them at constant risk. Also, if one was to say something that the king didn't like, look at or hear something they shouldn't, or look at someone in an unflattering way, that person could quickly lose his life. Thus giving us many low expressions for the mouth, ears and eyes.

- **아가리** [a-ga-ri] mouth, kisser or yap
- **아구창** [a-gu-chang] a diseased mouth
- **주둥이** [ju-deung-i] a muzzle, a bill or beak, same as **주둥아리** [judeungari]
- **귓구녕** [gui-gun-yeong] ear, also **귀싸대기** [gui-ssa-dae-gi]
- **눈깔** [nun-ggal] eye, also **눈탱이** [nuntaengi]
- **눈구덩이** [nun-gu-deong-i] eye socket, also **눈알** [nun-al] eyeball
- **콧구녕** [kot-gu-nyeong] nostrils, **모가지** [mo-ga-ji] neck,
- **손모가지** [son-mok-ga-ji] wrist, **발모가지** [bal-mok-ga-ji] ankle,
- **턱주가리** [tok-ju-ga-ri] the jaw, chin or chops, **싸대기** [ssa-dae-gi] cheek,
- **면상** [myeonsang] face, **낯짝** [nat-jjak] face or mug,
- **마빡** [ma-bbak] forehead, **이마빡** [i-ma-bbak] forehead,
- **대가리** [dae-ga-ri] head, **대갈통** [daegaltong], **대갈빡** [dae-gal-bbak]

Bodily functions
- **오줌싸다** [o-jum-ssa-da] to urinate
- **똥싸다** [ddong-ssa-da] to poop
- **방귀뀌다** [bang-gui-ggui-da] fart, also **방구** [bbanggu]
- **오르가즘** [o-reu-ga-jeum] orgasm
- **사정하다** [sa-jeong-ha-da] to ejaculate, also **싸다** [ssa-da] to ejaculate or cum
- **자위하다** [ja-wi-ha-da] to masturbate, also **딸딸이치다** [ddal-ddal-i-chi-da]

Children's language 쉬하다 [shi-ha-da] to pee, **쉬 마려워** [shi ma-ryeo-wo] I gotta pee (relieve myself), **응가하다** [ung-ga-ha-da] or **응가 마려워** [ung-ga-ma-ryeo-wo] have to poop (go number 2), **똥꼬** [ddong-ggu] butt hole (anus, cute)

Dirty Disease
- **병신** [byung-sin] a deformed or diseased person
- **지랄** [ji-ral] epilepsy, actual meaning is an act of madness, or calling someone on some bullshit in English (also ㅈㄹ for BS in English)
- **염병** [youm-byoung] typhoid (enteric) fever, a contagious disease

Evil-Ass Combinations
- **개새** [gae-sae] SOB short for **개새끼** [gae-sae-ggi]
- **쌍놈(년)** [ssang-nom(nyeon)] low-born bastard (bitch)
- **쌍놈(년)** [sshyang-nom(nyeon)] low-born bastard (bitch)
- **좆 같은 씨발 놈아** [jot gat-eon ssi-bal-nom-a] you dick-like fucking bastard
- **미친 새끼** [mi-chin sae-ggi] crazy SOB
- **씨발년** [ssi-bal-nyeon] fucking bitch
- **씹새끼** [sshib-saeg-gi] fucking son-of-a-bitch
- **빌어먹을 놈(년)** [bil-eo-meog-eul nom(nyeon)] beg-to-eat bastard (bitch)
- **호로새끼** [ho-ro-sae-ggi] & **호로자식** [ho-ro-ja-sik] bastard son
- **쪼다새끼** [jjo-da-sae-ggi] narrow-minded SOB

Beware of these words in translation

- 10 babies – becomes 씹새끼 [ssib-sae-ggi]
- 18 – becomes 씨발 [ssi-bal]
- 28 years – becomes 이 씨발년 [i ssi-bal-nyeon]
- Dog bird – becomes 개새 [gae-sae] SOB short for 개새끼

And for a little something new, try...

- Changhyun the Bitch 창현년 [chang-hyun nyeon]
- Son of a Siwoo 시우새끼 [siwoo sae-ggi]; that little shit, Siwoo 이씨우 [ee-ssi-woo]; Siwoo fucker 시우팔 [siwoo-pal]
- Fucking Peter 피터 [pi-teo] a spit of a swear in and of itself

A step further – slang or idiomatic swearing

- 좃까 없어 [jot-gga] literally "to peel a dick," and suggesting that you go get yourself circumcised, it means "hell no," "piss off," or "fuck off".
- 좃밥 [jot-bab] you insignificant dick (literally "your dick is (nothing but) rice"
- 좃되다 [jot-doi-da] to be(come) a dick, become spoiled
- 골빈놈(년) [gol-bin-nom(nyeon)] airhead bastard (bitch) or dumbass
- 물개이지 [mul-gae-i-ji] it's a seal, isn't it… slang for "of course, you SOB." An acronym for 물론이지 개새끼야 [mul-lon-i-ji gae-sae-ggi-ya]

Soft Swears – somewhat impolite but not too terrible

- 이씨 [i-ssi] can't believe it (somewhat similar to "bull" of bullshit)
- 이자식 [ja-sik] "you (little shit)" to a child, but "how dare you," to an adult
- 이놈아 [i-nom-a]; 이년아 [in-nyeon-a] OK for grandparents to say to grandchildren
- 제기랄 [jae-gi-ral] damn it, devil take you, gosh
- 젠장 [jaen-jang] shit (like shoot)
- 임마 [im-ma] again like "you little shit"
- 이뭐병 [i-mueong-mi] "what the hell is this (you fuckin' moron)?"이게 뭐야 병신아"
- 뭥미 [mueong-mi] a misspelling of 뭐임 [mueo-im] meaning "what the hell?"
- 멍청이 [mung-cheong-i] a blockhead, dunce or idiot
- 바보 [ba-bo] a fool, a stupid person
- 빵꾸똥꾸 [bbang-gu-ddong-gu] childish for fool, literally "fart-poop."

Off-swearing – swear sound-a-likes (as in dang, darn, shoot, fudge . . .)

- 씨댕 [ssi-daeng] or 씨밤바 [ssibamba] sound like *sshibal* [씨발]
- 씬댕 [ssin-daeng] darn or shoot
- 씹새 [sshib-sae] very close to *sshibsaeggi* [씹새끼]
- 멍텅구리 [mung-tung-gu-ri] idiot, like *meongchongi* [멍청이]
- 씨부리다 [ssi-bu-ri-da] what the fuck are you talking about?
- 빙신 [bing-sin] and 삥딱 [bbing-ddak] are softer versions of 병신 [byung-sin]
- 엿먹어 [yeot-meog-eo] lit. eat taffy, used to sound like 역먹어 [yeok-meog-eo] lit. "eat a swear word" and similar to "bite me," "eat shit" or basically "fuck off.

Index (Subject)

D

Index (The Big List of Slang)

Index (Slang Supplemental)

Culturally Speaking

List of Conversations

INDEX

249

INDEX

INDEX

251

Peter N. Liptak lives and writes in Seoul, Korea. An avid traveler and poet, Peter draws on Korea's people, language and culture as a source of inspiration, linguistic and otherwise. Keen on dialect and borrowed words in language, Peter did his MA in Korean Studies at Yonsei University. Catch up with Peter & his philosophical and poetic musings at CoffeeShopContemplations.com or PetesPoetry.com

A young philosopher who studied international management at KyungHee University, **Siwoo Lee** has taken a profound interest in the symbolism of language, combined with his fascination with foreign tongues and his sophisticated command of slang, has led him to delve into the world of A Rat's Tail.

See explanations of uncommon words and unusual usage.

Get the skinny on how Koreans think, speak and act.

Plus, how to pick up, break up, make up, or get down and dirty.

Find out who's teasing or abusing you and how to talk about them behind their backs.

Reviews

"This book is the bomb!" – Mr. Kim

"A must read for Koreans and foreigners alike!" – Mr. Park

"Shockingly fun!" – Mr. Lee

"Great bathroom reading!" – another Mr. Lee

CPSIA information can be obtained
at www.ICGtesting.com
Printed in the USA
LVHW06s0520220618
581563LV00014B/448/P